BOOMER'S

MIKE BOMGARDNER

ILLUMIFY
MEDIA.COM

Published by
Illumify Media Global
www.IllumifyMedia.com
"Let's bring your book to life!"

Paperback ISBN: 978-1-959099-21-5

Cover design by Debbie Lewis

Printed in the United States of America

Foreword

Michael Ivan Bomgardner, a.k.a. Boomer, and I first met as freshmen on the football field at Duke University in 1971. Boomer played on offense, I on defense. We "met" a lot during practice sessions and not in a cordial, congenial way. By the time we were seniors, we had become fraternity brothers, one-semester roommates, and co-captains of the Duke football team. Plus, we were pretty good friends.

One afternoon in late 2021, I was sitting on a couch in Boomer's Dallas area home. Boomer's wife, Barbara, a.k.a. BiBi to the grandkids, had just passed away a few months earlier. It was my second trip to visit since learning about his cancer diagnosis a few years earlier. I recall the way he broke that news. "They tell me that I've only got a couple of years left, but I bet I can double that, maybe even last five."

It was on that couch when I first learned that Boomer had been chronicling his cancer journey via Facebook postings. I was reading those exact words, asking him questions, and generally learning about an entirely different Boomer than I thought I knew fifty years earlier at Duke.

My singular thoughts at that time were that the words I was reading could be very helpful to others in similar situations. Maybe even those just dealing with life. That his shared journey, his faith, and Christian beliefs, so eloquently scribed, would likely be a very valuable gift to many.

I kept thinking; "His writings should be shared, published, made available to many. They are a gift."

Boomer's Gift.

Special thanks to Laura and her sister, Leslie, for translating the postings to a digital manuscript and making this project possible. Also, I sincerely appreciated the reviews and suggestions from Megan, Don, Gary, Jeff, Mark, and Kevin. Thank you all for your endearing friendship and feedback. Thanks also to Liz for pointing me in the right direction for publishing expertise.

Allie, Ivan, and Charlie, thank you for facilitating the sharing of your dad's words.

Most of all, thanks to Boomer. You continue to inspire!

Keith

December 2, 2019

As most of you have probably guessed I have been mostly absent on Facebook for reasons that really shouldn't need to be explained, but things have a way of changing. This past Sunday I heard a message from a guest speaker at our church (Dr. Jerry Taylor) who spoke about everybody's favorite subject: giving. It was a message that is moving me out of my comfort zone (safe place) and is challenging me to be more generous with the gifts, one in particular, God has given me. After a slow start in life, I have learned the blessings that come with faithful tithing and giving back in my late thirties, but Dr. Taylor drew a line of distinction between material giving and spiritual giving, pointing out that giving spiritually is much more valuable to God. He pointed out the obvious: we must take an inventory of our spiritual gifts, our spiritual wealth, before you can determine what he has placed in us to share with the world.

This past January the Lord gave me a gift that has impacted and blessed my life in unimaginable ways. It is my hope for those who are interested, to share these spiritual blessings with you over the coming weeks, months and hopefully years as I attempt to explain all the blessings I have experienced as a result of the return of my cancer. Tomorrow I will reveal the first blessing.

December 3, 2019

On Friday afternoon, January 25, 2019, Barbara and I stumbled out of my oncologist office having just learned that God did not answer our prayers and the cancer had returned. We were a little prepared based upon the response of our doctor's urgency following the scans that had just been taken. We had battled round one back in 2016 with surgery and twelve rounds of chemo and pummeled the cancer back into remission. I questioned my doctor about the treatment, and she said that like the last time I would take chemo every other week for forty-eight hours spread over three days. No problem, I've done this. But when I asked how many treatments this time, her answer was "until you tell me to stop." It only took milliseconds to realize that she was telling me that it was only going to be a two-round fight that was not going to end well. Then I asked what the average lifespan for people in my condition—two and a half years was shockingly abrupt.

This brought us to the most important questions that we would talk about and meditate on over the next day or so: What do we really believe? Is God who He says (and what we have been telling people) He is? Is heaven real? Did Christ really die for my sins? How could he do this to me, a so called faithful servant? All my life I have acted and believed I was prepared for any battle, but this was not win or lose or life or death. This was just death. As Barbara and I talked, wept, and prayed, we realized that *He* had already prepared us for this moment. God's faithfulness and presence in the previous challenges, opportunities, and spiritual development in our life led us to a better understanding of the first gift we must share. The gift of peace. Though life sometimes tries to threaten us, we truly have and are at peace with our God given circumstances. The things that keep me awake at night have nothing to do with my health. I haven't even googled colon cancer that has metastasized in the lymph nodes or explored miracle cures in other countries not bound by US law. I believe that God numbers our days before we are even born. That number hasn't and won't change. From day one we have leaned into our Lord, and he has comforted us with his peace. My prayer for all of you today is that you are experiencing or seeking God's peace.

December 4, 2019

I have been overwhelmed by everyone's response of encouragement and prayers over the last two days, some whom I have not had contact for decades. In yesterday's post I teased that today I was going to share the blessings of how God has prepared me for this season of life, but through your collective response, the spirit has moved me to comment on the gift of how cancer has transformed my practice and understanding of prayer. Since my baptism in 1991 (slow learner) I had developed a steadily improving practice of prayer. I am guessing that my church, work, and close friends and family would describe my prayerful interactions with them as pretty good. I am mostly comfortable praying in front of groups and have been fairly consistent in daily prayer.

What I learned this year was that when you have a terminal cancer, *prayer* is the only real tool in the tool bag. Chemo is undependable. Diet messes with your wardrobe. Exercise is difficult during a chemo week, and the dozens of "proven" holistic and alternative treatment suggestions are at best unsubstantiated. While I would like to believe that drinking seawater daily, taking water extracted turkey tail mushrooms from Japan, using dog deworming medicine weekly, or going to

Canada for highly concentrated extracted THC (pot) treatments will cure me, at the end of the day, it is only God who has the power to give me what is best for me (and you). There is a saying that when the only tool in your tool bag is a hammer, you see everything as a nail. When your only tool is prayer, you spend more time talking to God.

This gift of cancer has revealed to me just how undeveloped my prayer life had been. Before, whenever there was a challenge (or opportunity) at work or home, my first response was to jump in and fix or secure it. I turned to prayer, but it was mostly after I had failed. Often after hearing friends and acquaintances specific challenges or needs I would "promise" to pray for them. While I kind of mostly did pray for them, I must confess that far too many times the promise turned out to be hollow. Forgive me, please.

This year I have experienced how communicating to God through prayer opens a pathway for Him to communicate to me through the Holy Spirit as I give my needs and the desires of my heart to Him. Prayer has become a doorway to more fully sense God's presence in my life. I also covet and literally feel the prayers that you and others have offered on my behalf. I cannot thank you enough.

I wish I could say that I hear the Spirit and sense God's presence daily, that I have some supernatural connection with Him. I have experienced it enough that I believe He sends the Spirit daily, but I am the barrier that prevents me from the blessing of that daily experience.

In closing, my prayer for all of you today is that your prayer life has opened or will open a pathway for you to experience God's presence. Tomorrow I will share some of the ways that God has prepared me for this journey.

December 5, 2019

Yesterday was awesome, it was filled with unintended responses and reconnections with so many old friends. Sometimes we spend so much time in our own little sandbox, with our own little routines, that we forget to look outside at all the blessings God intended for us. You are all blessings, and as I have read (sometimes reread) your posts and looked through the names, so many great memories have been brought up.

We all have friends or family members that have experienced tragedy or hardship in their lives. Sometimes I watch and wonder, how can they get through this? Surprisingly I have seen many people go through this experience with a smile on their face and a spirit of trying to help or serve me, my family, and others through their difficulty. This is how and why I met the God of creation.

Many of you who have posted here knew me in my youth, and some of you are likely asking, "Who does Mike think he is fooling?" In the summer 1991 we moved back to Dallas to buy out my friend and business partner. I had never been a church guy, but Barbara twisted my arm, insisting that our young children needed to meet and play with people their age. Usually, I would have pushed back hard, but I was already deep in the doghouse, so I agreed. The first day at Sunday school, a family whose son had an inoperable brain tumor was giving an update. The father was talking about all the ways God had blessed him and his family the previous week. Later that day I met another family whose father, a fortyish-year-old policeman, also had an inoperable brain tumor. They had a similar positive attitude, discussing how grateful he was for a church that was helping them. I don't want to offend any of my former teammates, but these people expressed an inner strength that I had never experienced before. I was drawn to it and eventually gave my life to Christ and started learning—am still learning—what that really meant.

God prepared me from the very beginning for this season of my life. I could talk for hours, about the way God has shaped me over the past twenty-eight years. Some stories borderline on the miraculous but taken together, they are all about unquestionably divine intervention.

God's last reminder of who he was before I learned of the return of my cancer occurred the week between Christmas and New Year's 2018. The husband of our company CFO (Laura) had been battling with throat cancer throughout 2018. He passed away on December 28. I had offered to help with anything she needed, and she called me around 5:30 on December 30 saying that she needed to get the hospice bed out of her living room. She had talked to the driver that was scheduled to pick it up. He had informed her that he had seven other pickups in front of hers and that he probably wasn't going to get to her until after the New Year. She asked if I could help her get it out that night. She gave me the driver's phone number, and I gave him a call. I talked with him about how difficult his job must be—every delivery or pickup is for someone dying or dead—and I told him if he could pick it up that night there would be an envelope with $300 cash. He said he was on his way. We drove to Laura's house to drop off the envelope and discovered that she had not eaten in two days. We went to get her food. When we returned, the driver had finished loading the bed, and I confirmed that he received his money. Later, as Barbara and I were driving home, the driver called us. He said that his mother had recently died and that he had moved from LA a few weeks ago. This was a new job, and he had not been paid yet. Before I called, he had no idea how he was going to get home from work or what he was going to eat because he had no money. We talked about the mysterious ways that God works and prayed on the phone.

At that time, I was so grateful that God had showed me how he used the hardship of Laura's husband's death to take care of this young man, having no idea that he was preparing and reminding me that he will use my hardship to bless others.

My prayer today is that we will see and experience God's presence in our lives, even in hardship. It is there if we look for it. Tomorrow's cancer gift: my wife Barbara.

☆*☆*☆*☆*☆*

December 6, 2019

I have learned that when troubles come, you need something to hold onto, and the amount of time you need to hold on is mostly dependent on the severity of your trouble. For believers it's easy to say that we are leaning into our faith and holding onto the Lord (He is holding onto us), but the practice of our faith is often more difficult than the declaration. I also believe that even as we hold onto our faith spiritually, we also need someone to hold onto physically. It is no surprise that when we learned about the cancer's return, after forty years of marriage, Barbara and I grasped onto each other. There is no time to catch your breath when you get news like this. How and when do we tell our children, family, friends, work associates? What loose ends need to be tied up? Wills, business ventures, medical costs? How does this effect our bucket list? A few months back we had scheduled a two-week vacation that was to begin one week after learning of the cancer's return. It was to be a time with friends at our time-share villa in Cabo, but near the last minute, the friends coming for the second week had to bow out for their own medical issues. God worked it out for us to spend quality time alone together, isolated in a beautiful place so we could work through issues and adjust our direction. It was an exceptional week as we clung together praying, worshiping, weeping, planning, and laughing. This is where we rediscovered our joy and cemented our trust in the Lord. We were ready to come back and face reality.

Sometimes reality is more complicated than you can plan while sitting in a hot tub sipping tequila in a beautiful Mexican resort. Over time, we discovered an elephant hiding in the corner. We are headed down a path that is going to split. I have the easy downhill path, as I will most likely be headed to heaven first. Barbara, however, has the uphill path; at some point she will have to turn to others for physical and emotional support. We are not designed to live life isolated, and she will need to turn to her family and friends to replace our love and companionship. The responsibilities we shared will fall to her alone.

Fortunately, I picked a strong, loving, confident woman to share life with. I am not surprised, but I am humbled as I've watch her navigate the ups and downs of the last ten months with courage and tenderness as we work together to make the most of each day, balancing our needs along with the needs of our family and friends. Barbara has always been an active giver of love. She has demonstrated enormous strength, endurance, and patience as she has offset my weakness without sacrificing her efforts to love and support our family and friends. She is a gift from God that gets better with each passing day.

I have much more to say about how she and I have responded to the gift of cancer as I cannot fit into one note.

My prayer for all of you is that you have or find someone to spend time with to make the gift of tomorrow special.

December 9, 2019

This past weekend I learned that I may have to communicate that I am not doing very well or am even close to death. Though none of us are guaranteed tomorrow, I currently feel great. If it were not for chemo, I would feel perfectly normal. It is hard for me to believe that I am even sick, but I know that the scans and blood tests are real.

Back in January, having learned of cancer's return, as Barbara and I stumbled back to our car, we were already reviewing the things we were going to need to address. One of many was our bucket list. I had re-retired the previous July, and we had amazing travel plans. They included several multi-month vacations to Asia and South America along with many shorter trips throughout Europe, Egypt, and maybe return trips to Africa and Israel. When you are given a limited window of time it is amazing how your priorities change. Suddenly trips were replaced by important things like seeing your grandchildren start school or graduate from, well, anywhere.

The things on your bucket list are interesting. They not only represent what you value, but they occupy your thoughts as you think about how long you will stay, what you want to do, and who you want to go with. As you go through life, you get to check them off one by one and start thinking intentionally about which one you want to check off next. Recently I realized that I had neglected to include the destination that is far and away the most important trip I could ever make. I had left heaven off the bottom of my list. While I have discussed heaven often with friends (I even taught a men's Bible study on Revelation), until recently I wasn't really planning or getting excited about making the journey. Believe me I am not ready to rush off this earth prematurely. I am not ready to leave the people I love, and I still believe that Lord has plans for me here. However, I must admit that when the time comes, I will not miss the neck, back, shoulder, or knee pains when I get the new body promised by our Savior.

Is heaven at the end of your bucket list? If not, why? Is there anything you desire more? Even if you grew up disbelieving in God or were perhaps pushed away by some uninformed supposed Christian sharing judgment or hate instead of love, why would you not want to explore heaven again

My prayer today for all of you is that your bucket list is full and that you can finish it completely.

December 10, 2019 (1 of 2)

Continuing with the bucket list: Yesterday I wrote about how we plan and prepare our bucket list. We start with expectation, pick out the most important experiences. We know that to get the best results, we cannot wait until the last minute; you must start the ball rolling early. Yesterday I wrote about my final bucket list, the perfect ending event—heaven, an eternity with our Lord. A trip like this is not to be kept to yourself; it is best shared with loved ones. We felt that our children were not really pursuing our Lord. If I know anything, it is that you cannot really tell all that is in someone's heart. If everyone else is like me, we are not really fit to judge anyone, well, except maybe our children.

As Barbara and I prepared to share my new medical condition with our children the first time, we anticipated their first question, and when they asked "what can we do?" we replied that there was only one thing we would like them to do: go to church with us on Sundays followed by a free lunch on me. Our daughter, Allie, replied that they were attending a great church off Legacy in North Plano, Chase Oaks. I said great, we will alternate between Chase Oaks and Valley View Christian, our home church.

The initial result of this *new life* approach is evident through our granddaughters as pictured on my Facebook cover page. It has also led to some interesting, deeper, more spiritual conversations with our children.

Over the past seven days of writing, I have been so blessed by the words the Holy Spirit has given me. He has shown me that my journey is more about you than it is about me. As I stated above heaven is best shared by loved ones. Who are the loved ones you want to share heaven with? Can you identify them by name? Are they ready if Jesus calls them home? Are you? When should you do something about sharing your eternal love for them?

My prayer for all of us is that we can share our love with our family and friends eternally.

December 10, 2019 (2 of 2)

My children each year ask me the same question. After thinking about it, I decided to give them my real answer.

What do I want for Christmas? I want you! I want you to keep coming around. I want you to bring your kids around. I want you to ask questions and for you to ask for my advice. Tell me your problems. Ask for my opinions. Ask for my help. I want you to come over and rant about your problems, rant about your life, whatever. Tell me about your job, your worries, your fears, your wife or husband, your kids, your fur babies. I want you to continue sharing your lives with me. Come over and laugh with me or laugh at me. I don't care. Hearing you laugh is music to my ears.

I spent the better part of my life raising you the best way I knew how, and I think I did a pretty darn good job. Now give me the time to sit back and admire my work. I'm proud of it.

Raid my refrigerator, help yourself, make yourself at home. I really don't mind, in fact, I wouldn't want it any other way.

I want you to spend your money making a better life for you and your family. I have the things I need. I want to see you happy and healthy. When you ask me what I want for Christmas, I say nothing because you've already given me my gift all year. All I want is you!

December 11, 2019

Recently I realized that the return of my cancer was actually an indirect answer to prayer. In our lives we have all witnessed and experienced end-of-life circumstances. We have seen people taken instantly. I had a younger business partner that acquired an infection and died in a few days. He was a good man and friend but left his family in a state of unpreparedness. We have all watched people with Alzheimer's or dementia living with little purpose or understanding while their loved ones struggle to take care of them and deal with the burden of knowing real conversations and love-sharing events will be few or none. For years Earl Campbell, the once great running back, has been crippled, mostly confined to a wheelchair. If you have recently gone through or are currently going through one of these scenarios, I have compassion for you and pray that I am not adding to the burden of your day.

Over the years, as Barbara and I have encountered these types of circumstances, I have shared with her that I prayed that I would have a different (better) exit path. First let me confess that cancer was not what I was asking for. Right now, I feel great, but I look around the room while taking chemo and see some who are struggling and imagine that this will not always be the case. But even right now while I do feel great, I know that I have been blessed with quality time that has and is enabling me to finish unfinished business with and for my family and friends. As a result, I can only conclude that my cancer may not be the gift I wanted—compared to alternatives—but it is the gift I needed. I praise God for all His gifts and will continue to praise Him in all circumstances.

I am headed to the infusion room to take off my pump as I have finished another round of chemo. Please pray that the medicine is doing its job and containing or shrinking the cancer cells. Thank you for all for your encouragement. I pray that in whatever you have gone through or are going through you will encounter God's presence and will praise Him.

December 12, 2019

Over the past two weeks, I have heard from so many dear old friends (no emphasis on old). You have no idea how much you have lifted me up. I have been like a little kid, checking to see which new names popped up today and who was checking in again. With each name there is a memory attached, and these memories make me smile and replay so many fantastic events that I have been blessed to share with so many of you.

Through all this renewed communication, I have discovered that I may have created some confusion related to my current health and thought today I would clarify. In late January of this year, we learned that the colon cancer we fought in 2016 had returned and metastasized in my lymph nodes. The medical classification for this is stage 4, but if you had asked me to score how I felt at the time, I would have given an 8.5 out of 10, discounted for the lower back pains, shoulder pain, and some knee swelling—mostly related to my short-lived football career. Today as I write this, I am an 8.0 but expect to move back to 8.5 over the next two days as the chemo leaves my body.

During this period, I have had four scans. The first scan in January established the baseline, and the second scan in the April showed actual shrinkage from January. My body has historically underproduced platelets and coming out of the April scan my doctors recommended reducing the chemo quantity by half and eliminating one of the drugs that puts stress on the platelets. The next scan was in August. During that period, between the second and third scan I missed three complete treatments due to a low platelet count and received only 50 percent of the typical chemo regiment. This scan revealed that again there was no growth in the lymph nodes but showed some small additional growth in the lungs, nothing above 5 millimeters. My doctors have resumed giving me 100 percent of the typical chemo treatment, which they feel should reduce or hold the line on the growth in my lungs.

I am feeling great and for a point of reference, in September Barbara and I did a three-hour hike in Colorado at ten thousand feet of elevation. We will likely all face difficult times ahead but today the struggles we face are more spiritual than physical. Currently my journaling effort is to help examine and confront the spiritual challenges we face. Overcoming our spiritual challenges have eternal consequences while our physical issues are temporary. If something changes health wise in the future, I will share it with you. Thank you again for your prayers and support.

My prayer for all of us today is that we might fully understand our spiritual challenges and who we need to turn to in order to overcome them.

December 13, 2019

As I end the second week of posting I thought it might be fitting to add a little levity and share a story with a miraculous ending that reinforced my belief that God is in control and has a sense of humor. Warning: this story could be painful for my loyal Duke family.

On November 26, NCAABB power Stephen F. Austin visited the No. 1 Ranked Duke Blue Devils at Cameron. This game was supposed to be a stat sheet filler and confidence booster for the young Devils. But what happened that night turned out to be nothing short of miraculous on several different levels. Duke haters everywhere cheered as SFA, a huge twenty-eight-point underdog pulled off the miracle win in overtime, but there is much more to the story.

Nate Bain, a senior forward from the Bahamas scored the winning basket in overtime. As it turns out, Nate's home was destroyed in 2018 when a hurricane not only took his house but also his father's church. After getting approval from the NCAA, SFA's athletic department created a GoFundMe page for Nate and his family, and prior to the game they had raised about $5,000. When Nate's family story emerged following the game the site was overwhelmed with donations from Duke haters and Duke lovers alike as nearly four thousand people blew past the $50,000 goal to raise more than $150,000.

This is a great story, but according to my wife it was a miraculous answer to her prayer. In the spring of 1977, during my first date with Barbara, we were trading the typical "get to know you" questions about family, places lived, and work history. Barbara shared that she was a teacher, and I asked her where she went to college. She told me she had graduated from Stephen F. Austin. I was relatively new to Texas and was not familiar with SFA. I asked her if SFA was accredited. She was not amused and immediately started firing questions at me in retaliation.

Eventually I gave her the opening she was looking for as I shared that I went to Duke on a full scholarship. I think she had sized me up well and knew that it was probably not academic. She asked what kind of scholarship. When she heard football, she had the opening she wanted. "Football!?" she stated. "No offense but I never dated football players." I asked why and again she responded with a huge grin on her face, "No offense but you know football players just aren't that smart." I smiled back and told her, "That's okay, I never dated blondes."

It took forty-two patient years of waiting for a miracle, but her prayer was answered, and she finally received justice.

My prayer for you this weekend is that if you have been waiting and praying for some unanswered circumstance or injustice to be healed that you will give it over to our Deliverer. He will answer your prayers.

December 15, 2019

Tomorrow, Monday, December 16 is our forty-first wedding anniversary. I am writing today so I can give Barbara my attention tomorrow. I was thinking that forty-one years is quite a measurement of time, and my mind took me down a slippery path of all the ways we measure time, both backward and forward. We celebrate the past and measure time annually with anniversaries, birthdays, New Years', Christmases, Easters, Independence Days, Memorial Days, and many others. Our office even celebrates the first day of the NCAA basketball tourney. I wondered which of these measurements of time capture the most meaning or value as I examined my life to date (slippery slope), and which might give the most value and meaning going forward.

We most likely all have different answers, personal ways of examining the past and anticipating the future, but this is my post and you're stuck with mine until you examine your own.

Anniversaries: Any couple that has survived forty-one years of marriage has two warriors. Marriage can be hard at times and brutal at others. I am blessed to have a warrior wife that at times has single handedly kept our marriage together. She is a testament to God's grace and is God's all-time second-best gift to me. The more I consider it, however, I am not sure that just measuring your time married together is the very best barometer. I recognize that there is nothing that I am prouder of than my marriage and my family, but the idea of enduring for decades together is just not enough. When you consider the number of unsuccessful marriages (I had a failed starter marriage myself), it generates a very uneven baseline. I know that we will only be separated by death but as I look forward to anniversary forty-two, forty-five, forty-eight, or whatever, with some uncertainty, just using the number of years that we were together to measure our life together is inadequate.

Measuring your birthdays is fun. It is Hallmark's excuse for a party, but I hate to look back and realize how many cumulative years I've wasted with procrastination, bad choices, and selfish living. Even now, as intentional as I am trying to be, some days I look back and see empty efforts. Although, I must confess that looking forward, participating in the birthdays of Barbara and all our loved ones, has become significantly more important.

New Year's for me is historically the most disappointing and un-fun Hallmark holiday.

Christmas and Easter are not about us, they are *for us*. They have eternal purpose, and, quite honestly, I still struggle to fully comprehend the width and depth of God's love for us. How can we measure even one hundred years on earth when compared to an eternity in heaven.

So how can we or should we measure time? As I continue to dwell on understanding this complex concept, I am leaning heavily toward the most important measurement of time: the moment we are in. I believe the journey of our lives have carried us through the struggles and victories of the past to prepare us for the moment we are in right now. How should we measure what we do next?

Tomorrow, I intend to honor my wife by spending the day with her, pampering her, and reminding her that she is important to me. My prayer is that by doing this I will also honor our Lord who put us together. She is truly a gift from God.

My prayer today and tomorrow for all of us is that we will recognize the gifts our Lord has shared with us and that we will honor Him for those gifts.

December 17, 2019

When events go from easy to very difficult, it is always educational to see who steps forward. Who will be among the first group that charges up the hill, steps forward to even out a fight, or runs to the aid of someone in need. First responders have their title for a reason. They have earned it by turning their training, courage, and responsibility into actions. Most of us have our own first responders, the people in our lives we can trust to step forward in our time of need. I plan to take a few days to write about the blessings and the ways that my trusted army of warriors has responded.

As a parent there is no greater joy than watching your children handle difficult circumstances and unite to serve and protect your family. As I shared the information of the vengeful way my cancer had returned, I was reminding them (and maybe me) of our faith and trust in the Lord. I said that "Our lives are in the Lord's hands" and that "I believe our days were numbered before we were even born and that having a little more information doesn't change the number." For a moment my daughter, Allison, forgot who I am and what she heard and that I was just going to turn everything over to God and not pursue treatments. She became angry and was in my face saying, "You have to fight this." The next week she and her brother Ivan were in my oncologist's office grilling her on the status of my condition and wanting to know the battle plans.

Generals know that when you go to war your need a supply line to replenish your battle resources and weapons. The doctors replenished my chemo every two weeks but all my children (including spouses and our newly, legally adopted son Charlie) replenish me daily with emotional support, prayer, encouragement, and often their very presence with the grandchildren. The chemo breaks me down and my children lift me up. I know they pass up social opportunities with their friends, evenings of rest, and opportunities to take care of many of the things they need to do to make the thirty-plus-minute drive to spend time with me and Barbara—to help replenish us the most important resource they can give: their love.

I am also aware that this is not just a battle for me and Barbara but also for them. During this past year we have watched the unexpected blessings of my cancer draw them all closer together. They are both physically closer as Ivan and Leah have moved into the same neighborhood as Allie and Dusty. Charlie has also moved just down the road to be closer. They have literally circled the wagons. We have also watched them circle the wagons spiritually as together our family is leaning into our faith. It's a great gift that most likely would not have occurred with the return of my cancer. Can I get an amen?!

My prayer for all of us today is that as we face the troubles of life, we will not let them blind us from all the blessings taking place around us.

December 18, 2019

I woke up this morning about 3:30 thinking and eventually praying about what I would post today. I was already planning to do a short series on the "angels" God has already put into my life as well as the ones he continues to add. I laid there meditating next to my sleeping wife for almost two hours before I finally realized that I was not going back to sleep and might as well get up and write. I have been blessed throughout my life by being surrounded by good, strong, supportive "angels," but as I started contemplating the various friends and groups of people, I realized that it was a virtual army. I was also reminded again that I am a slow learner as I realized that all of these "angels" that God has sent are just everyday people like you and me.

When your world finds out that you have cancer, it is truly amazing how many people (angels) come to you with recommendations or personal stories about how to fight to win. I determined early on that I was not going to grind on all the medical, dietary, and spiritual remedies available on the internet and that I was going to trust God to put the right doctors, dieticians, and pastors in place (or He could just heal me outright). To date I have never even googled the type of cancer I have. Besides, we all know that the internet is just a place you go when you want to find information that supports your own personal beliefs because it is filled with contradicting truth. Honestly, I know I am not smart enough to analyze and determine which treatments would be the best for me anyway.

Fortunately, I already had an angel in place. Donna has been our friend for more than forty years. Barbara and I have vacationed with her dozens of times, including trips to a mission trip to Israel and a safari in Tanzania. She has been in the medical field all her life and while I have never fully understood exactly what she did, she did it well enough to retire very comfortably in her fifties. So, when the word spread that my cancer had returned and the recommendations for treatment started rolling in, she volunteered to analyze them all and get with Barbara to determine their recommendations. This was an enormous undertaking. There were recommendations to go for treatment in Canada, Cuba, Mexico, Korea, Japan, and literally dozens of locations within the US. Dietary recommendations were all over the board (oncologists don't really weigh in on dietary recommendations). Apparently, hundreds of people have been cured drinking fresh sea water daily, ingesting high concentrates of liquefied pot, taking water extracted turkey tail mushrooms from Japan, utilizing a regimen of canine de-wormer, and taking a combination of dozens of vitamins and supplements. Donna not only analyzed all of these but has also searched the web for other potential remedies, treatments, and trials. She has lifted a huge burden off Barbara and me. She is an angel, a heavenly gift.

Have you examined and identified the angels that have been put in your life? My angels include biological family, church family, work family, neighbors, friends from school, and *you*. Please do not underestimate how significant you are to me and Barbara. When you have something that your doctors admit they cannot cure, the only real medicine is prayer, and I don't need an angel to analyze that truth. My challenge for us today is to spend some time praying and meditating on who, besides me, might identify you as one of their angels and to recognize and give thanks for the angels God has already placed in your lives.

My prayer is that as you do this you will be uplifted as I have been.

December 19, 2019

Previously I shared how Barbara and I leaned into each other and into the Lord together when we learned the cancer had returned. We knew where our hope was centered, and that God ultimately has a plan for us. We just didn't have a good idea what that plan looked like. I think we knew that it would involve some method of demonstrating our faith in our Savior, but this was new territory for us, a once-in-a-lifetime opportunity—when you might only have one chance to get something right, and you don't want to blow it. We (me a little more than Barbara) were ready to put ourselves "out there," but where exactly, I wasn't sure.

Then an angel appeared in the form of Allison (best Economic Development Director in Texas) who shared a story with me about her friend who went through cancer, and she gave me a copy of the book he wrote titled *Out of the Blue*. I highly recommend this book for families and people dealing with cancer. At the time Barbara and I were packing for two weeks in Cabo, a last respite before starting my chemo treatment and a perfect opportunity to read a book. Right now, my former teammates and fraternity brothers are snickering in disbelief that I would read a book. Fortunately, it was a short book with big print and the author, Greg Murtha, who ultimately died from cancer, told his story about what he called "a life interrupted." He spent his final years on the lookout for people who were struggling with life, trying to be sensitive to their needs and *stopping* everything to encourage them with prayer or to meet some physical need. He defined these divine appointments as interruptions that God had placed in his path. He looked for them, and he found them. I found it inspiring.

As King Solomon said, "there is nothing new under the sun," and as one who never struggled with plagiarizing good ideas, I thought that this is what I will do. Then the Lord sent another angel to meet me in Cabo. Sitting on the edge of a cliff, overlooking the Sea of Cortez, looking for breaching whales with a beverage in hand, I started up a conversation with the family in the lounges next to ours. Interestingly, the family reminded me of the one I grew up in. As I shared my condition and my faith with their twentysomething daughter, Kayla, took interest and started asking questions. As it turns out she was raised by non-believing parents disinterested in pursuing their faith, like me, while she was serving full time in college ministry at Penn State. That first day we talked for maybe two hours as I shared my testimony with her and her parents. I don't know if her parents or brother were moved at all by the conversation, but she was grateful because she shared that it had been difficult to have that conversation with them. Later in February, I Skyped into her student group in Pennsylvania to share my story. This connection gave me confidence and directed me to a different path than the one taken by the author Greg Murtha, but a path that leads to the same destination.

The Bible describes the way to heaven as a narrow path. Perhaps that is because we all have our own road to take and each of our paths is just wide enough to carry us individually to our anointed destination. My prayer for everyone today is that we have or will find our path, the one that leads us to heaven.

December 20, 2019

A little over nine years ago my company was in the market for another salesperson, and my younger partners came to me and wanted to hire my daughter, Allie. This was well after we had worked through her teenage (I know she was possessed) and (selfish) college years. Our relationship was fully restored, and I could see no upside to the idea of us working together. I was well known internally for making all the girls and some of the men cry with my passionate management style and had already generated all the tears I would ever want to see from Allie. But apparently it was her lifelong dream to have a role at Innovative (she had worked some summers and holidays), and she lobbied my partners hard. This created some real conflict as I was used to getting my way at work and Allie was used to getting her way with me. It turned out that my partners were right, and she is an awesome salesperson, managing our JC Penney and At Home relationships.

Yesterday in the office, like most workdays, we were having a talk about her twin daughters and upcoming events (Christmas, family ski trip in March, extended family wedding and Disneyland in Southern California in May). Barbara and I had already committed to a very generous Christmas, covering the expense of three days at Disney, and had been discussing the cost of ski school in March along with after-Christmas Ski clothes shopping for the grand girls. Usually, I am the one trying to cut back on the excessive spoiling of our children and grandchildren, but this time it was Barbara saying it was too much. As I was interrogating Allie about her plan for ski clothing for the girls and throwing Barbara under the bus for her stinginess with our grand-daughters, without thinking about it I said, "you know your mother may have twenty or more years to spoil you, but I may have only a hand-ful." I had never really thought about this concept. If I had, I might have been sensitive enough not to verbalize it in front of my daughter. As the tears streamed down her face, she asked for a hug, and we spent a few minutes holding each other and weeping together.

I have had about twenty hours now to think deeper about this concept of time and spoiling the people around me. This has led me to two conclusions.

First, there is no way that I will hold back any future blessings on my wife or my children and their children. I have no doubt now that I have stated this publicly that they will milk me for even more. That is their nature, which they inherited from me. I am good with it.

Second, I believe that this is the way our Lord thinks about us. He has already thought about our future and how he is going to spoil us with His heaven. Like Disneyland to a child, it is a place of unimag-inable glory. He has already prepared it and offers it to us freely. The question is how will we respond? Or more importantly, how will you re-spond? In the same way I want my children to "milk me" (tried to think of a better metaphor) our Lord wants us to grasp *all* the riches He offers.

The blessing of living through this journey with cancer has moved me to a place of deeper, spiritual understanding and anticipation of what is waiting for me, for us. It fills me with *joy*. It makes me feel the way I picture me and my granddaughters sharing Disneyland together, all dressed up in our favorite costumes as we run from event to event. Heaven is not only better when shared with the ones we love, God also designed it to be spent with Him.

My prayer for us this morning is that we can shake off the burdens of this world and experience the joy and anticipation of what is waiting for us.

December 22, 2019

Back in April of this year, as a city councilman (Farmers Branch, Texas) I was a failed supporter for the construction of a new library for our city. I remember seeing an online post from opponents suggesting that my motive was to leave a legacy. At the time I remember thinking that my accusers must not understand that I had already accomplished things of value well beyond the support and construction of a building. Recently I have been confronted by this idea of leaving a legacy a few times and have lost a little sleep reviewing the things of value in my life to date. I considered the idea of having a building, statue, or road named after you, but recent events confirm that concepts of greatness are like fashion, they go in and out of style. History is littered with men and women who were honored in their generation but have somehow now turned into villains as well as those who were labeled as quacks in their time but later have been recognized as being ahead of their time. Apparently, a legacy can be honorable or dishonorable at different times or even at the same time.

I wondered if the retail support business I cofounded back in the early eighties and that has survived and thrived through tumultuous conditions and technology changes might qualify as a legacy. Over more than three decades I have watched our sales associates get married, buy houses and new cars, have children, raise their children, and send them to college (several have already graduated). I have watched multiple former employees leave and start their own businesses. I have also watched as many of our customers and manufacturers succeed as we partnered to grow their businesses. When I retired it was the successful relationships with all the people that I was most proud of. But is this a legacy? As my younger partners have been buying my stock over the past few years, it is their leadership that is driving the success, and we have added six employees that I barely know to our Dallas staff alone. If this is my legacy, it is already fading.

I am still mulling over the idea of a legacy, but for me, it will be my family. I believe that all parents want to watch their children surpass them in life, and I am proud that my children are already way ahead of me at their current stages of life. They may or may not start businesses or make more money, but their quality of life and the values they live by took me decades to learn and understand. Like me, they all picked quality spouses with shared family values. I remember a few years ago when my son Ivan was looking for a job and passed up an opportunity because the next promotion would take him out of Dallas. It was his action that gave me an understanding of the value of our family being together. He taught me.

More importantly I have four grandchildren who are mostly perfect. We spend time together weekly (sometimes daily) and not just at major events and holidays. Yet, while we are blessed today, our hope for the future is that this legacy will become our children's legacy and eventually our grandchildren's legacy. Our parents have been gone just a short time in the big scheme of things, and yet we don't celebrate their birthdays or anniversaries anymore. They are not forgotten by us, and yet they are not remembered by our grandchildren.

And still, I believe our legacy will be passed on through our belief in Christ. The Bible makes clear the importance of generations, and we will be united in heaven with previous generations and Christ followers we don't know yet. This is an offshoot, a vine, of the greatest legacy of all time, Christ. He is the focal point of our biggest annual holidays. We get together and celebrate him weekly and try to speak to Him daily in our prayers. He gave us the tools (love, forgiveness, sacrifice, self-control, grace, peace, hope) to graft our family, the family of Christ, together.

December 24, 2019

What are you hoping for this Christmas? We are trained before the moments we even remember to hope for our perfect gift. Our parents, family, and friends ask us what we want, and we spend weeks thinking about and hoping they will come through. Gift givers hope that their thoughtful gifts will bring joy to the receiver, often struggling to find that perfect gift. Moms are hoping that the turkey will turn out great and there will be plenty of food to send home leftovers for everyone. We hope for beautiful weather, maybe even some snow and maybe that your crazy Aunt Mary will do something even crazier this year.

If you think about it, there is no other time of the year that is filled with as much hope as the Christmas season. I believe this is not happenstance. As Hallmark, Macys, and Amazon may seek to exploit our hope for their own personal gain, the truth is that this has been the season of hope for a couple thousand years, and it is designed for *our* gain.

While many of us hope for extravagant gifts, others hope they won't be alone this Christmas and that someone will remember them. Others hope for a new or better job so they won't get evicted from their home or can buy something nice for their loved ones later after they have saved a little money. Or you could be hoping for a new kidney for your husband or maybe that your spouse or parent will be sent home from the hospital before Christmas. I also know that I am not alone in my hope for a cure or healing for my disease or yours. Still others are hoping for forgiveness from some friend or family member for some past discretion or to find a way to give up the bitterness you hold against someone who has hurt or disrespected you in the past.

You don't have to have an obvious malady to be hoping for something that is outside your own ability to correct. We are all dealing with something that steals our joy. What is it for you? Betrayal, fear, uncertainty, a missed opportunity, death of a family member, divorce, drugs or alcohol, children issues. Where can we find our hope, find our joy? These are the real reasons we celebrate Christmas, to remember that Christ came to live among us, to show us where to find hope and to experience full joy. It is through the struggles, experience, and troubles of our everyday life in contrast with the peaks and highlights that we have witnessed that demonstrates what is *not* available to us under our own strength and plans. It is in the short, complete, perfect, loving, painless moments of our existence that we can identify the beauty and desirability, the promise, and the *hope* of heaven. And it is in the imperfect, conflicted, painful, unforgiven, unloved, decaying, procrastinating, needy imperfect seasons in our life that clarify our need for *help*.

Christ came to give us both *help* and *hope*. *Help* in the form of a roadmap to overcome the obstacles that stand in the way of perfection and *hope* for an infinite eternity living in the presence of God.

The real challenge for us is, do we trust the roadmap? Will we read and follow it? Do we understand the significance of the gift Christ is offering? I must admit that there was a vast time in my life when I did not even consider the gift, let alone take the time to read the roadmap. I have learned that it is never too late to pick up the map (I was thirty-eight) and my gift of cancer has taught me to slow down and reread the map to help me identify and share the experiences along the way to my final destination.

My prayer for all of us this Christmas is that we will take a first or another look at Christ's roadmap for us and spend as much time remembering why we celebrate Christmas as we do on how we celebrate.

Merry Christmas!

December 25, 2019

A few weeks ago, as we were talking about our Christmas plans, Barbara realized that this would be her first Christmas without any of her parents. (Her dad passed away this past July.) Then she said something that got me thinking: "This will be Dad's first Christmas in heaven." As we celebrate Christmas today down here, what are they doing up there? How big is their tree? December 25 is the day we have chosen to celebrate; do they match ours or use the real date? When you're living an infinite number of days and years do you even bother to number them? Is Christmas more important than Resurrection Sunday? I have this silly picture in my mind of Christ walking into the great hall described in Revelation and holding his scarred hands up victoriously as all of heaven rejoices. I am not trying to be blasphemous; it is just that my feeble little brain cannot begin to comprehend how glorious and holy it will be. Maybe we won't even celebrate Christmas and Easter but will celebrate the date Christ left earth and returned to heaven.

I believe it is more likely that every day will be like Christmas and Easter rolled up in one with more glorious, daily celebration and rejoicing, singing, and worshiping than anything that any of us have experienced here on earth.

My prayer on this fine Christmas Day is that all of those who are missing loved ones they have recently lost, as we have, can take some comfort knowing that regardless of whatever we are doing down here, they will be doing it better up there. My prayer for everybody is that we will open the gift of Christ once again, or maybe for the first time, with anticipation and excitement.

December 27, 2019

On a Sunday morning in mid-October of 2010, Charles Otto Dodson was sleeping soundly on his brother's girlfriend's parent's couch. It was the third or fourth place Charlie had found to crash following an encounter that took place a few weeks earlier when his father arrived at their apartment drunk with a new female friend in tow and announced that since Charlie was eighteen and was receiving his mother's social security check, it was time for him to move out. Family dysfunction was a way of life for Charlie. His mother had died when he was a very young child (he has no recollection of her), his father was an alcoholic, and his older brother had turned to drugs. It was not uncommon for his family to get evicted from their apartment. He once had taken Barbara around to some of the places he had lived before. At one building he described coming home from school and seeing all their possessions on the curb. People were grabbing things and walking away. His older brother and friends would get high and taunt him. I cannot imagine which is more frightening for an eighteen-year-old boy still in high school, staying put in an abusive household or being pushed out the door with no certain direction. Sadly, he didn't have a choice.

On this Sunday morning life was getting ready to change for Charlie. He calmly describes being awakened by a voice that said, "Go to church." He rolled over and looked around, seeing no one he went back to sleep. Then he heard the voice again. Like most young men Charlie was a slow learner, but this time he got up and followed the mysterious voice's direction. He got dressed and walked to the closest church. When he arrived, he only recognized one face, Eric Quintanilla, an El Salvadoran refugee that had been raised by our good friend Mary who took him in when he was just a young boy (he was the nephew of the woman that cleaned her house). Hearing Charlie's story, Eric invited him to stay with them and Mary agreed. Eric and I had been cooking award-winning "Lake of Fire" chili at our church's annual fall (faux Halloween) Festribration Chili Cookoff for several years, and I met Charlie when Eric invited him to join our team.

As it turned out, by mid-January, Mary, a single professional woman, was overwhelmed trying to manage her work and support both boys. She came to Barbara and asked her to pray for a solution because she did not want to be the next person in a long line of people that had rejected Charlie. We became the solution. Barbara and I were already in a relationship with Charlie through the chili cookoff and sitting together at church on Sunday mornings.

We met with Charlie and Mary and talked through all the details. It was agreed that Charlie would finish high school with us and then go off to the Army (he had already enlisted). Our children were great. Ivan tutored Charlie in math. Allie taught him to dance and provided his girlfriend one of her old prom dresses. We got him into a driver's education class, and our friend Colonel Steel (retired Marine) trained Charlie for basic, teaching him to shoot and clean the guns he would be using and getting him in shape.

It was mid-spring when we learned Charlie was in the Army Reserves, not the Army. He graduated, went to basic and combat medic school, and then came home. Once again, we were no longer empty nesters. Charlie became part of our family, and though he got to a place where he moved out and was self-sustaining, he never really left; we adopted him spiritually. He called us Mom and Dad, and our children referred to him as their brother. Charlie was grafted into our family in the same way we are all grafted into the body and family of Christ.

Upon learning of the return of my cancer, following discussions with Barbara, our children, and Charlie, we legally adopted him on October 18 of this year. He is in the process of changing his name to Bomgardner, and we will be planning a celebration shortly after that is completed. The Bible tells us that all "who overcome" will get a new name from the Lord (Revelation 2:17, 3:12). My son Charlie is an overcomer.

My prayer for us today is that we will all be "overcomers "in the eyes of the Lord.

December 30, 2019

As we close out 2019 it is reasonable to review last year's resolutions before pushing forward with 2020, but for some reason I have been distracted and cannot even remember what last year's resolutions were. They probably had something to do with my weight, diet, and exercise. If so, I did okay (great at times early in the year) on everything but exercise, but I had a little unplanned help. If you're like me, looking back, most of my past resolutions were *all* about me and my health, wealth and entertainment. None of them were really a big deal. They all could easily roll over to next year.

This year I have been rethinking my approach. Though my ego still pushes me to look trimmer, taller, and healthier, I am changing my focus. As I sit here this morning receiving my last chemo treatment of 2019, my resolution for 2020 is simple: I want to *live*. While this might seem obvious—what good is any resolution if your heart is not beating—my goal for this time next year is not just to be alive, it is to be *full of life*, abundant life.

As I look around the infusion room this morning and think back over my twenty-one visits this year, I could identify only a few people who are living a life of expectation and anticipation of how the Lord is going to bless them tomorrow. Looking back on the experience of 2019, I see it was overflowing with unexpected blessings. We celebrated the expectation and delivery of my first grandson, Michael Ivan Bomgardner (a.k.a. Spike, as named by the twins). We enjoyed our first Bomgardner family reunion in twenty years not motivated by a wedding or funeral. We attended church consistently with my children and their children and had numerous visits from great friends for dinners. We had to start saying no to because we were so booked. We adopted Charlie, and I experienced a plethora of divine appointments and opportunities to share my faith, not to mention the inspiration to write these accounts of my experiences and blessings attached to my journey with cancer.

Once again, the Lord provided abundantly for me (and my family) in 2019. What does he have planned for 2020? Part of my resolution is that my eyes and ears will be open to see and hear all the wonderful experiences and opportunities God has prepared for me and that I will be ready to seize each one of them as they confront me. This coming year I want to be ready with the words and courage to share God's *loving* truth to my family, friends, and anyone else I meet. My resolution includes saying *yes* to more invitations and spending more time with my family and friends, as much as my body will allow.

Wednesday morning (January 1) Barbara and I kick off the year in Cabo. We're spending seventeen days with some friends and family. I have no idea how consistent I will be in writing these posts over the next couple of weeks but should have some time to share my blessings.

As 2019 goes into the history book, my prayer for all of us is that we can and will enter 2020 with anticipation and excitement for the fullness of life that is coming our way.

January 7, 2020

Today, January 7, at about noon, as we cruised along the shores of Cabo San Lucas, we had one hour left in our half day fishing trip. So far, it was empty (no fish). Without thinking I just said a little prayer, Lord we need some fish to cook tonight. Then I realized that this was the first time I had talked to the Lord since we got up at 5 a.m. As I thought a little more, I realized that the last several days had been pretty much prayer-free. During the previous four weeks, as I took time to construct these posts, I have spent significant time praying and listening and have never felt closer to my Maker. Then I come to Cabo with some friends and in less than a week's time stumble off my path. Why are we so easily distracted and misled? Why does God put up with our ungratefulness and unfaithfulness?

For the first time in dozens of fishing excursions in Cabo we got shut out and didn't even see many whales that are usually everywhere this time year. Do I think that the Lord was punishing me by withholding fish and whales because I had forgotten about Him? Absolutely NOT! I do, however, believe that the Lord uses circumstances to encourage us to return to Him because He loves us. I also believe the more resistant we are to his subtle reminders, the less subtle He is likely to become in showing us how much He loves us. He works in mysterious ways.

I pray that your "spiritual year" is off to a better start than mine and that all of us will take the time to invest in our relationship with our Lord.

Since we have no fish to cook, we are off to grab some food in a spot that has a great sunset view. God's spectacular design will be on full display.

January 11, 2020

Continuing with events that shaped my life, in August of 1968 my family packed up and moved from Wichita, Kansas, to southern New Jersey, a suburb of Philly. I was going into my sophomore year of high school, and this was the seventh time I had moved. In Kansas the bad kids were drinking beer, and I didn't know any of them. When I got to New Jersey, virtually everybody I met, including most of the athletes, were already drinking, many of them liquor. It was my first conscience experience with negative peer pressure, and I folded like a pup tent in a hurricane. By Christmas I was mixing whisky into 7Up bottles to fit in. Even though I became a well-known athlete in the area, I never felt accepted. I felt socially awkward throughout high school. My friends from Duke and later in life find this tough to believe, but I never had a girlfriend for prom and only one for homecoming through my three years of high school.

At Duke, I adjusted socially, but I still felt like an outcast academically and financially as most of the students came from wealthy families, at least by my standards. I only got in because I was an athlete. I was just a dumb jock. (My wife even implied it on our first date.)

Why was it so hard to feel accepted? Why did it even matter? While I made some fantastic, lifelong friends along the way, why was I willing to give up so many of my values just to be liked, just to fit in? There were times when I wanted to be like people that I didn't even like. Why did it take so long to discover and accept what my true value is? Were the adults in my life trying to teach me this, and I was just a slow learner? Perhaps they suffered from the same lack of confidence and personal understanding, unable to teach what they didn't know. Who should be responsible for teaching young people this critical information, and is there anyone teaching the young people today?

When I re-examine my life, there is only one consistent source instructing us about our true worth, teaching us where our value comes from. I took me almost forty years to identify the source, and I am still learning how to apply the teachings. That source is our Creator, and the teachers are His followers that use His textbook (Bible) to explain the nuances, layers, and depth of His words. Unfortunately, many teachers today try to interpret His Word in light of the culture and in doing so discount the value the Creator intended for us. As each generation in America seems to slip further and further away from God's teaching, so does the value of life.

This gift of cancer has caused me to closely re-examine the value of my life. Looking back there are plenty of events that were just not very pretty, but my Creator determines the value. He sent His Son to die for me on a cross. This was a life-changing event because I learned that my worth did not come from what people around me thought of me; it came from what God thought of me.

My prayer for all of us on this fine Saturday, is that we will discover and understand our true worth.

January 14, 2020

As I have continued mentally exploring the unplanned events that shaped my life, I've realized that it is not just the events, it is the people in the events that seem to multiply the impact. In my last post I wrote about peer pressure in a negative sense, but I believe that much of the progress in my journey out of "boyhood" is a direct response to trying to meet a higher standard expected by the people around me, my wife, business associates, neighbors, and family. If bad company corrupts good character, then good company must have the opposite effect. And when you go through challenges together with "good company" it changes you; it has changed me.

In August of 1968 we left Kansas and moved to New Jersey, just in time to start fall football practice. I was just a sophomore and ruffled a few feathers by working my way into a starting position at linebacker as the new kid. We had some really good players on that team, but our record was 2 wins, 7 losses, with no conference victories. Not surprisingly we had a new young coach the following season, Coach Horner. Virtually all our key players from the previous season had graduated, and we were picked to be cellar dwellers again. We embarrassed the prognosticators by going undefeated, winning our state group. (New Jersey high schools were separated into four groups by size. We were group 2, the second smallest.) At the end of the year we were rated the best team in southern New Jersey for all groups. We repeated those accomplishments the following year.

This was my first experience with the impact of real leadership. I had many coaches growing up, good and bad, but Coach Horner had something else. It wasn't just X's and O's; it wasn't just technique or organization skills or preparation. It was something more. He fostered a culture that is difficult to describe. It was a combination of what all coaches want their programs to be—a loving, supportive family—but with him it was real. It was also fair, a term not used to describe many coaches. He was passionate but not angry when dispersing discipline. He was a motivator. He also planted the first seed in me to become a Christ follower, though I rejected it, once again demonstrating that I'm a slow learner.

Outside of my father he was the first man that I remember wanting to be like, and as a result I did something seventeen-year-old boys seldom do. I listened to him. He is a reason that I ended up at Duke (my second choice was Vandy), and he is the reason I was prepared for football when I got there. He still coaches and keeps up with my teammates today.

While I learned many other things from many great people along the path through college and onto my business career, the culture Coach Horner created is the one I tried to develop in my own career. He demonstrated that just one person can have a significant impact in a team, business, or any organization. Coach Horner changed my vision of what was possible and though I have failed more times than I would like to admit, he influenced me to strive to be a difference maker.

My prayer for all of us today is that we have "coaches" in our lives that challenge us to be our best and encourage those around us to be the same.

January 15, 2020

In mid-December of 1981, Barbara was pregnant with our daughter, Allie. We had a contract to sell our condo, and Barbara was zeroing in on a house. I was a furniture buyer for Joske's Department Store and the only internal candidate for a promotion to merchandise manager. The week before Christmas I received a call from one of my furniture manufacturers who informed me that they had given the job to a buyer from another department store who was less experienced and less qualified than I was. I marched into the VP of personnel's office and asked for an explanation. His response was less than acceptable, and I was pissed! I had worked hard for that position. I had been a leader in sales growth and profit in my current position and in my three previous buying positions. Now I would have to wait out the failure of this new person or start preparing my resume. It was the first time in my life that I did not get the position I was fighting for. If I had been a Christian at the time I might have called out, "God why have you forsaken me?" (maybe a bit overdramatic).

We all have those moments in life when we think we have earned, deserved, or just expected something to go our way. We look for someone to blame. I blamed the VP of personnel who once confronted me about my pricing and product strategy, which earned me the biggest promotion of the year while I was the bedding buyer. He forced me to defend myself in front of the rest of store management in a way that made him look foolish with the results of the promotion.

This turned out to be the best thing that ever happened in my professional life. On December 26 I got a call from a good friend who said he had a line of video game cartridges (Atari) and was going to start a manufacture's rep company. He needed a partner in Houston. He offered me partnership in a new company, calling on customers between New Orleans and Laredo, Texas. We would have to move—take my wife and coming child away from her extended family. We would lose our insurance (Barbara was pregnant), and I would have to bankroll myself until we started receiving commission checks. If I had been offered the promotion at Joske's, there is no way I would have jumped in with my friend Tony (not Cabo/fishing/neighbor Tony).

This disaster of getting overlooked for the promotion led to a business (Innovative Sales Group) that has blessed me with nine different partners over the years and dozens of employees. I have learned that when disaster occurs, I need to start looking around for the opportunity or blessing that God is getting ready to reveal to me.

When People ask me how I can be so positive walking through this experience of cancer, I tell them that I am looking for, and finding, the blessings and opportunities all around me. Cancer, like other disappointments in life, is just one door closing and another door opening, and I don't want to miss the opening door.

My prayer for all of us today is that we don't focus so much on the struggles of life that we miss the blessings and opportunities taking place all around us.

January 16, 2020

One of the consequences of being in a military family and moving frequently is you typically end up spread out when you become adults. My family covers all four time zones. My sister, Debbie, lives in New Jersey. I live in Dallas. My brother Mark lives in Colorado, and my brother Steven lives in Washington State. As a result, the only times we really get together are at weddings and funerals, and even then not everyone seems to make it. We all have a very strong sense of family but most of our efforts seem focused on our children and grandchildren, as it should be. We have a very close—as close as you can have while being separated by thousands of miles—relationship and unlike many families, we *enjoy* spending time together. We just hardly ever do.

One of the blessings of cancer is that now they cannot just blow me off when I invite them to spend time together. When they have tried to, I play the cancer card and remind them that "this may be the last time you get to see me."

I know that this is a manipulative approach, but it is very effective. I coerced twenty-six family members, spanning three generations, to meet us at the beach for a week last July and was able to get my brothers, sister, and sister-in-law to meet me in Cabo this week. From what I remember these were the first times we have all been together without a major event since we went to Disney World together a few decades ago.

We have spent this week in Cabo together, and though we have an odd collection of different political and spiritual beliefs, we have a bond that supersedes all conflicts. Despite our differences we are unified in the belief that nothing should separate or come between our love for each other. This gift of cancer has drawn us closer together and for that I am grateful and thankful.

I believe that this is the type of relationship our Lord desires with us. The challenge is that though He is fully committed to the point of sharing His Son on the cross, many times we let our personal circumstances and struggles get in the way. Instead of letting our difficulties separate us from Him, I believe God wants to see us respond to these challenges by drawing closer to him. This is the gift I have been blessed with since the discovery of my cancer's return.

My prayer is that we can all get to a place where we might understand how our immediate challenges and circumstances are an opportunity to draw closer to our Creator.

January 17, 2020

We moved back to Dallas in the summer of 1991, and Barbara, claiming that our children needed to meet new friends and interact with children their age, convinced me to attend a local church with a summer camp for young children. I had absolutely no interest in attending church, but men often do things they really don't want to for their children and to keep the wife happy. Something happened at that church that moved me to become a Christian, but that's a story for another day. That's when I started a journey that transformed me into who I am.

When I first gave my life to Christ, I really had no idea what that meant. I was ready to accept His gift, but I was not sure how we were to respond to His teachings or share my gifts. One of the men that discipled me, Weldon, was always challenging me to get out of my comfort zone. He would ask me to do something that seemed outrageous to me, like pray out loud in front of people and pray for people I didn't know. I was a thirty-eight year old professional who was used to leading meetings and discussions, but when they asked me to be the president of our Sunday school class, which involved taking prayer requests and praying aloud, it was frightening. Looking back, I don't know how I made it through the year. It never seemed to get easier.

One Sunday in the late spring of '92 Weldon said that the church needed several thousand dollars to replace some carpet and asked me to pray for someone to step forward. Barbara and I had already responded to the teaching we had received on giving and were generously giving as much as fifty dollars a week on most Sunday's. At the time I was frequently entertaining business customers and would never have considered buying a bottle of wine for less than fifty dollars. I was a slow learner. When I prayed for someone to step forward with a few thousand dollars, I felt an unexplainable urge to respond. I talked about it with Barbara, and we wrote a check after the service. What happened next was mind blowing to me.

At that time, I was preparing to buy my partner out and was working seven days a week. That Sunday afternoon when I went to my office, both fax machines (the precursor to email for you young ones) were ringing and beeping because they were out of paper and the memory was full. Purchase orders had spilled out of the containers designed to catch them and were littered across the floor. On the weekend the primary fax machine had never run out of paper, let alone both of them. It had never happened before, and to my knowledge, never happened again.

Some people might consider this a coincidence, but I have experienced too many similar blessings to accept it as happenstance. I think I have mentioned a few times that I was a slow learner, but this lesson was clear to me. The blessing was not in the purchase orders I received but rather in the understanding that I needed to listen closer and work to put the teaching into action. This took place more than twenty-five years ago, and I am still amazed by how much I still need to understand and act on. It was a turning point in the development of my faith.

This gift of cancer is teaching me a whole new set of lessons about how I can share the gifts God has given me. My prayer tonight as I write this post back in cold, rainy Dallas is that we might reexamine how we respond to Christ's teachings and God's Word and explore the things we should be giving God praise for and the ways we should respond.

January 20, 2020

In 2006 Innovative Sales Group shipped north of $200 million to CompUSA. They were far and away our biggest customer and represented half of our company's total revenue. Our company structure was built around supporting their merchandising and marketing needs. We had nine people (including three partners) dedicated to managing our business with them, which included products from more than thirty different manufacturers. In May of 2007 they closed their stores and liquidated all their product, leaving us with a ton of unanswered questions. Questions like: How can we replace the lost revenue? Which of our other customers have the most potential for growth, and do we have the right people in the right places to support those opportunities? How many people do we need to let go and who? Those are easily the most difficult and heartbreaking decisions any business owner will ever make. My younger partners and I discussed and prayed about the issues regularly. Dragging our feet, we were reluctant to make changes as we searched for answers. We ended up laying off one person, our receptionist, Nikki.

We decided that we would wait for a few months before making other moves. We reduced the partners pay plan and continued to talk about what changes we would need to make. While we were waiting (and working), the Lord answered our prayers with what can only be described as manna from heaven.

Some friends from another business like ours but focused on different customers connected us with a Korean manufacturer called Digital Steam. To my knowledge they had never shipped anything to the US previously. They had no market penetration, no brand name, and their infrastructure in the US consisted of flying over a salesman with no US experience and an engineer for meetings when needed. They were launching one product, an analog to digital TV converter box. This was when all broadcasts were moving to digital, and the US Government was supporting this change with a thirty-dollar mail-in rebate. Our largest remaining customers—Walmart, Sam's Club, and AAFES—were only planning to dabble in the technology, viewing it as a short-term play because all future devices would incorporate the digital features.

Fortunately for us Radio Shack viewed the category as a major opportunity and liked Digital Stream's pricing and application of the technology. Over the next two years they sold more than 4 million units and continued to sell large quantities all the way up until they filed for bankruptcy in early 2015. Radio Shack took virtually all the product Digital Stream could manufacture and aside from a few small shipments to smaller retailers never delivered any other products to the US.

Like the manna from heaven provided by God to the Israelites as they fled Egypt, this opportunity just fell out of the sky and landed in our camp. It sustained us while we worked to grow our businesses with our other retailers and allowed us to launch a Seattle office to address the opportunities with Amazon, Apple, and Costco. By the way, we re-hired Nikki, the receptionist we let go, and she has worked her way up through our company to become one of our best salesmen, managing Craftsman, Stanley, Black and Decker, and Conair at The Exchange (formerly Army, Air Force Exchange Stores-AAFES).

As I continue to look back at the unearned blessings that our Lord has shared with me, it reminds me of the lyrics from the Michael Bublé song "Home": "It's like I just stepped outside when everything was going right." It is my personal experience that reinforces my desire to search for the blessings in the difficult times of life like cancer, to find the beauty in the ashes.

We all have "ashes" in our life. My prayer for us today is that we don't miss the beauty.

January 26, 2020

Have you ever felt compelled to do something sacrificial to help someone else, knowing it was the right thing to do, but then later you find yourself in a difficult predicament and wonder, "How did I get here?" We have all heard the expression "no good deed goes unpunished" and perhaps you have experienced it, maybe more than once.

In September 2015 our church had an after-school tutoring program for elementary children. On Mondays and Wednesdays, we would give fifteen to twenty children a snack, some gym time, and then work with them on their homework and educational development. Barbara and I volunteered to support this noble program, and I reluctantly admit that Barbara's teaching credentials overpowered my contribution.

On Wednesdays we would invite children living in nearby Section 8 housing and also feed them. Unfortunately, this had some unintended consequences. This infusion of young, largely undisciplined students created an enormous disruption in the programs as they spoke out of turn, frequently fought, or just wrestled, and sometimes intimidated other children (regular church members) in the program. I personally was proud of the commitment our church made to these young people even when it created a situation where several member families left for more traditional teaching environments for their children.

There was one boy I'll call M that was exceptionally disruptive and drew his friends into unacceptable behavior. After counseling him several times, I decided the best thing to do was remove him from the room. We sat in the hall and read the first chapter of Proverbs together. I told him that Proverbs was written for him and pointed out verse 8 where it says "Listen, my son." I told him many of the other chapters had a similar reference.

I knew that this boy was in trouble and felt the Holy Spirit calling me to intercede, but I suppressed it. The next week was a repeat of the previous week, and as we sat in the hall reading chapter 2 of Proverbs, I felt the Spirit again and felt compelled to act. I explained to M what a mentor was, what the responsibilities of a mentor and mentee were. I told him I was willing to try it if he was ready to make a commitment. He said he was, and we came to an agreement. I also told him that I thought we should include one of his friends (safety in numbers) and asked him if he had someone he would like to include. He chose C, and that night after class we invited him to join us.

We have been on this journey for more than four years and together we have experienced so many emotions, teaching moments, learning moments, failures, successes, disappointments, and hope. Despite raising our own children and believing I was ready to take this on, I learned I was (and still am) unprepared, naive, selfish, and at times, uncompassionate.

(Later, I will share more about how the Lord used my ego and arrogance, along with my desire to be faithful, to place me in a situation to transform me while I was still believing I was going to be useful in leading and transforming these young boys.)

As my cancer has pressed me to examine my relationship with my Creator, I have come to see with more clarity (not to be confused with clearly) that the circumstances God has prepared for me are designed to draw me closer to Him, to improve our one-to-one relationship. I also believe that God uses people like me, and other circumstances, to draw you closer to Him. And finally, I believe that God uses people like you to create circumstances to draw others close to Him.

Lord, please give us clarity on your design for our lives. Draw us closer to You and use us to draw others closer to You.

January 27, 2020

When M and C agreed to join me in this mentoring experiment, we started learning about each other. M was in fourth grade, and C was a year older, in fifth grade. Neither had dads living with them; one was in jail. They both had older brothers and moms that loved them but struggled with virtually every aspect of life. M struggled to go two weeks without getting sent to the principal for fighting, and academically their goal was just to pass the annual testing that would keep them out of summer school. They were both smart, but like most young boys with little supervision they spent most of their time playing and challenging what little authority existed. They lived in Section 8 housing surrounded by families just like their own. One of the first things I noticed was that they had few identifiable role models. It did not take long for everyone to know that I was investing in M and C, and whenever I pulled up to their apartment to pick them up, my car would be surrounded by children asking me to take them too. I learned what I already knew: the need is great, but the workers are few.

We agreed on a schedule to meet twice a week when I was in town. I continued to work with the boys on Wednesday nights, and I would pick them up for church every Sunday morning with donuts and kolaches. Following church we would meet and talk about the sermon, explore some related Bible passages, and then we began our quest to find the best burger in North Texas for Sunday lunch.

Sounds simple but the details are always in the execution. Many Sunday mornings when I came to pick them up at least one of them was still asleep, and sometimes one of them had gone to spend the night at a friend's house and wasn't even there. Sometimes nobody answered the door. As recently as last Monday I had made plans to pick up C for a late lunch following my chemo. When I showed up at his apartment, his mom redirected me to a friend's apartment at a location they used to live. When I got there, I received a text from C directing me to a different address. When I got there I realized that he did not send the apartment building and number. Clearly these boys didn't understand how important and valuable my time is? I know the Lord has been testing me to see if I will give up.

Additionally, sometimes I think they think that I am Santa Claus. They need clothes for school, new athletic shoes (do they have to grow?), balls, books, gifts, and more. Yesterday it was a catcher's mitt and a baseball bat for C. They come to me for things they need but sometimes it is difficult to differentiate between what they need and what they want. Another test? (For clarification M moved more than twenty miles away more than a year ago which has prevented us from continuing.)

They need education. Every time we meet we talk about school, reading, grades, behavior, and relationships with teachers and friends. C was struggling with math and science, so we hired a tutor to work with him on Sunday afternoons. This was extremely effective and had a huge impact on his grades and confidence, but he didn't show up about one out of five times—usually when I was traveling. I still had to pay the tutor—yet another test. There are plenty more tests which I will save for a future post.

The truth is that I have failed some of these tests. I must confess that at times I have searched for the Lord to release me from my commitment, but it is just another prayer that has gone unanswered. I do believe that I have helped M and am helping C, and the Lord is using me to improve the trajectory of their lives just by sharing my testimonies and using the gifts he has already blessed me with. At the same time, He has made it clear to me just how blessed I have been in virtually every facet of my life, things that I have traditionally just taken for granted or thought that I earned or deserved. These boys don't deserve any less than me, and I have not earned any more than them; I know too well my sinful nature.

This experience continues to challenge me in many ways and expand my understanding of God's design. For that I am extremely grateful.

Lord, help us to accept and work through the details in our life that just don't go the way we want them to, or the way we would design them, so that we might experience and learn the life lesson that you have prepared for us.

January 31, 2020

Yesterday afternoon I picked up the film from my CT scan and the radiologist's written recap to take to my doctor's appointment at Houston's MD Anderson Cancer Center. I could not resist opening it up and taking a peek prior to the appointment and was surprised when the first statement on the paper said the imaged thyroid gland is unremarkable. Throughout my life I have worked (and failed) tirelessly to avoid being unremarkable. The term *unremarkable* was used three more times in the report, and as I read it, I started having flashbacks to my freshman English class at Duke. Clearly this radiologist was not cognizant of my sensitive nature and ego. As I searched for some thread of positive recognition, I finally found the term *remarkable* used in two separate sections to describe the degenerative disc disease throughout the thoracic and lumbar spine. I can't imagine where that came from.

The report was good but not perfect. Everything was stable except for four small nodules in my lungs that grew between one and four millimeters (the largest was only nine millimeters). Everything else was the same size (small) and nothing new was reported.

The plan going forward is basically the same with the addition of one of the traditional drugs they had backed out of my treatment about six months ago. I feel blessed that I get to continue living fully and freely for the foreseeable future yet, even with the minor growth. I am also reminded that I am still dependent on my Savior to determine the circumstances of my remaining time here, to heal me, hold me, or take me. I am comforted by that.

Regardless of what comes next or when it comes, my life has been remarkable. It has been filled with challenges that helped unite me with the most fabulous collections of people as we worked together to overcome the obstacles and opportunities of life. While success was often evasive or fleeting, even in failures I have been blessed beyond imagination by the relationships formed during the battles. At some point of my life, I have participated in at least one of these ventures with many (most) of you and am honored by your work ethic, determination, partnership, and friendship, regardless of the outcome. We have pushed each other to be our best and I thank you for making me better.

Today, the thing that excites me most is that I am (we are) not finished. I know most you who are following these posts, and you are remarkable, not just based on what you have already done but also what you still can do wherever you are and whatever you're doing.

My prayer for all of us today is that in the future, when we look back on this period of our life between now and then, that we will describe this next set of experiences as the most remarkable to date.

February 1, 2020

This past July Barbara's father passed away, and she wanted to get a new dress for his service. It was a chemo week, and I was riding with her as she pulled into the narrowest parking space available, the wheels of both cars were on the lines. As I was struggling to get out without dinging the car next to me, I was aggressively confronted by an angry black woman. She was literally screaming and waving her arms as she approached me acting like I was wearing a KKK uniform. It had not been a very good day or week, and of course I responded in an unemotional, apologetic, non-confrontational demeanor, eventually. But first I needed to defend my wife and myself. She accused Barbara of hitting her car but as she examined her car all she could find was a tiny hairline scratch on the back of her mirror. She was still yelling, demanding our insurance and drivers' licenses. I attempted to explain that if we had hit her mirror the scratch would be on the front and not the back. I also explained that the scratch was so small that waxing her mirror would remove the mark. She was still in my face threatening to call the police. Barbara was trying to get between us, to protect me, but I think the woman took it as an aggressive action and amped up her tone, if that was possible. It was a combustible situation that had attracted a small gallery of onlookers.

There are many types of heated confrontations, and my bet is that we have all been in more than just a few. How it turns out depends on what you do next. Over time I have learned that in these circumstances the best thing to do is seldom the thing you want to do. We were at the point that the next escalation could only include violence. This time I did something rare. I took a step back, and she stepped forward. I shared with her that our week had been tough, and we were here to buy a dress for Barbara's father's memorial service. She stepped back and acknowledged that she also was having a tough week and was in the process of moving to Dallas. I asked if I could pray for her and within minutes, we had exchanged information about our struggles and had our arms around each other as we wept and prayed together.

What are the confrontations in your life, and how are you responding to them? Are they continuing to escalate? Are you plotting a course of action to gain superior positioning to take out your foe? Are you arrogant about your moral or intellectual advantage? Are you willing to compromise your values or character to "win"? Will you gloat? If you are losing, are you prepared to fight to the death? We have so many choices and ways to get into the fight, and we get so emotionally amped up that we forget that in all these conflicts we can choose *peace*.

Interestingly enough, the Bible informs us that people who choose peace are wise and those who choose conflict are *fools*. I wish I could say that I have never been the fool but that would just be another lie that I would be telling myself. Which side do you come down on?

Sadly, we live in a time where so many people in our country are just itching to get into a fight, and we are a nation divided along political lines. We have not been this divided since that civil war. My questions for all of us is: Are we going to fight? Or are we going to pray? Are we going to push, bully, and pound those that think differently? Or will we put our arms around each other and look for agreement? As a Christian I believe that God is in control. He anoints and deposes leaders (presidents, dictators, kings) at His will. Our choice is to get behind Him or plant our flag behind one of the self-serving, lying, despicable politicians (an accurate description for both sides) that are working to divide our country.

We should not fall for the lie that our country is doomed unless we are all prepared to line up behind these *fools* (just using the biblical definition) that want to lead us into internal conflict. Our country is not going to fall apart in the next ten months and then we get to choose our next leaders. We have an effective system in place to work through all this that is monitored and directed by our Creator. We should not follow these *fools* from either party down any path that wants to change our constitutional system and rights.

I pray that we will trust in God, trust that He put the leaders in place to mold and lead our great country in the beginning, trust that He and He alone remains in control today, and trust that like any father He wants what is best for us. My prayer for you today is that we would choose peace over winning at any cost. This is what I believe.

February 3, 2020

I met with my primary oncologist this morning to get her reaction from my scan from last week and her recommendation on this next season of treatments. Her response was virtually identical to my MD Anderson consultant's last week. She too was unimpressed by my cancer's growth. Apparently, I am not just unremarkable but also unimpressive. It seems like all these doctors (like some politicians) are very comfortable picking on defenseless old men. Like all the other challenges in my life I am learning to just live with it. Medically, the net effect is that I am getting a larger dose of chemo today (currently being infused), and depending how my body responds, they will add an additional drug in two weeks. With a little luck I will be even less impressive in the future.

I have been thinking about what I can be doing to improve my health, and I keep coming back to diet and exercise. After a great start in the first three-quarters of last year, over the past four months I have completely lost my discipline to make good food and exercise choices. I gained twenty-five of the fifty pounds I lost. Last week as I was meditating on my metamorphosis to becoming "unremarkable" and recognizing my lack of discipline I started thinking about my "old" teammate and friend Alvis Vaughan. He recently won a national bodybuilding competition for men over sixty (check him out on Facebook), in fact, I think he has won many competitions. It is remarkable to consider the discipline Al must have to keep his body in championship shape as he approaches his late sixties.

How are some people able to focus on a goal and achieve incredible results while I swear off excessive sugar to help fight my cancer and still had to have some blackberry cobbler last night at 10 p.m. (for the second night in a row)? I am reminded of Romans 7:15 where the apostle Paul writes, "I do not understand what I do. For what I want to do

I do not do, but what I hate, I do." If only I could isolate my failure of will to just diet and exercise. In the end (I hate to start a sentence this way) we are all blessed to choose who we want to be and what we want to do, and the only thing holding us back is us, our inability to follow our own will.

If we cannot even follow our own will how much more difficult is it for us to follow our Lords? Fortunately, in the same way we give ourselves grace when we fail to do what we want, our Father in heaven also gives us grace when we ask. In both instances grace gives us the freedom to start, and even fail, again and again.

My prayer for us today is that we will all recognize the freedom we have through God's grace, and despite our past failures, we would double and redouble our efforts to follow God's will for our lives.

February 6, 2020

This past Monday my oncologist increased my chemo dosage in our effort to further slow additional growth or hopefully shrink my cancer. Typically, the night of my first day of chemo is sleep challenged, I think it is a reaction from the steroids that accompany my medications. So, this past Monday I was up until about 2:30 a.m. watching the Iowa caucus returns mixed with State of the Union address and impeachment rehashes of rehashes. Even that did not put me to sleep. The last time I looked at the clock, it was 4:07 and then I found almost four hours of sleep. For the past couple of days, I have been resting and watching our political system at work (?). I have started to write my political opinion on several occasions only to delete my post as I neared completion. I do not want my political opinion (or yours) to diminish the message of God's grace or the power of our testimony to change lives. But every time I try and dismiss it, I feel the Holy Spirit tugging on me to speak out about Gods authority in this conflict of opinions.

Does anybody besides me feel like our elected leaders generally act like a bunch of third graders? There is name calling; bullying; ripping up someone else's work; joining a gang (party); tattling; making up stories to scare the uninformed or make their opponent(s) look greedy, uncaring, or power hungry. While this has been ramping up for the past decade or so, these last few days have been a display of historical pettiness and both sides appear to be following their juvenile performance by doubling down with more impeachment, more Hunter Biden, and more pronouncements of the imminent demise of our great United States as the moral justification for taking action. While both sides say we must do this now to save our great nation, in reality they are driving the country farther apart.

Like our forefathers, I believe God raised up this great nation and blessed us with brilliant moral leaders. These leaders established laws and a constitution that protect us still today. Our nation is built to survive poor leadership because we are a free people, and we regularly have an opportunity to change our leaders and have demonstrated we will fight for our freedom (many of us are well armed). There is no chance that any president could become a dictator or sell Alaska to Russia. This is typical fearmongering. Our citizens want more political turnover (term limits) not less, and this past week is a clear example of why we need it.

Our political parties act like gangs. They hold up corporate America for money to run their campaigns. They stake out territories (gerrymandering). They find a way to skim enough money to make themselves very rich by the time they leave office, and there is no room for a moral compass. While I disagree with one of Mitt Romney's votes, I do not chastise him for making it. We need more (some) politicians on both sides that can work together on a moral basis to continue to protect our country and advance our quality of life. Our politicians are dividing us into mobs that feel free to say anything or do anything they please.

When you find out you have cancer, or some other intrusion on the quality of your life, you know it is time to circle the wagons and start praying harder and praying together. Our nation has the beginning stages of cancer, and Trump, Pelosi, Nadler, McConnell, Schiff, Giuliani, and the press are not the disease, they are just the symptoms. We have lost our way as a nation. We no longer trust in God. We no longer enforce or trust our laws. Without God we will lose hope, and without legal structure (laws) we will continue to slip further into chaos.

I am guessing that I have probably stepped on a few toes. Please know that my intent is to invite you to step back, take a breath, and remember the history and character of our great nation that has been blessed by God from the very beginning. The sky is not falling!

Lord, I pray that you will give us ears to hear and eyes to see all the blessings you have planned for us.

February 15, 2020

Last night Barbara and I invited nineteen of our friends to a Valentine's Day dinner at our house to thank them for the love we have all shared together, in some instances for decades. This is one of several groups of people we share life with that has a record of actively supporting us in the trials we've faced and celebrated with us in the victories. We have also walked with them through the ups and downs they have experienced. Altogether, we have overcome (because we are overcomers) the sadness caused by death, dementia, cancer, and MS along with the disappointments of our children's (and our own) poor choices, job loss, divorce, and other private struggles that are not my place to share. We have also celebrated weddings, promotions, anniversaries, new grandchildren, and retirements. This morning, as I think about it, the collection of last night's group of friends and the challenges we have faced together fits many of the different groups that have sat at our table—family, neighbors, church, work, school (Duke and TCA), sports teams, and all sorts of groups.

The truth is life is hard. It's filled with pain, struggle, disappointment, sorrow, loss, rejection, failure, and disease. Worst of all, life is not fair. "He causes the sun [success] to rise on the evil and the good, and sends rain on the righteous and the unrighteous" (Matthew 5:45). That is why we need support and encouragement from our friends. Somehow Hallmark has highjacked this concept, first introduced to us in Genesis 2:18: "It is not good for the man to be alone." I think it is interesting that even while God walked with Adam in the garden—before death, disease, and sin—He knew that we needed help. I think it is appropriate for Valentine's Day that we celebrate the gift of our helpers though it would probably be more appropriate to celebrate them more than once a year. Our dinner table holds a maximum of about twenty people. That does not even begin to cover the number of "helpers" God has put in our lives, and I would like to thank all of you for the way you love and care for me and Barbara.

My prayer tonight is that the people we all share life with look to us when they need support and encouragement because they know from experience that they can depend on us.

February 16, 2020

Last Tuesday I wrote about feeling like I was at a crossroads, standing between some previous priorities which were or were not on their way to being accomplished and identifying something new to invest in that I could find passion for. I have been chewing on this subject for almost a week and have been led to Ephesians 2:10: "For we are God's handiwork, created in Christ Jesus to do good works, which God prepared in advance for us to do." The Lord is maintaining my health, so He must have some "good works" planned for me. As I mentally explored what type of work that might be, I zeroed in on my current circumstance (cancer) and these writings which I have felt led to share. Perhaps the Lord has bigger ideas for my current path.

Several people have suggested I should put these writings together and write a book, but the fact is I barely have the patience to read a book let alone write one. I also believe that the impact of anything I might write, even if some people believe it is good, will only last about a week after my memorial service. Recently several people have reached out to me "offline." I have had some dialog, mostly superficial, regarding some things they were going through. I feel the Spirit nudging me to go deeper, to explore the struggles they are enduring, and share some perspective that might help them with their struggle and their relationship with Christ.

This path is frightening to me. First, I have no moral authority to counsel anyone. I have failed almost all the ten commandments and am still far from living sin-free. Many of you have known me for thirty to fifty years. When I look back that far, I don't even respect myself. I was literally the guy the Bible warns about in 1 Corinthians 15:33. Additionally I have no formal biblical training outside of maybe twenty-plus years (baptized in '92) of attending church and Sunday school and participating in small groups. Yet, I have a strong sense that this is what the Lord wants me to do. So, I am putting it out there.

Galatians 6:2 tells us to "ear one another's burdens" (NKJV). Thank you for your support in bearing mine.

My prayer for us today is that anyone needing help in bearing their burdens will reach out to someone they can depend upon and share their need. Of course, we all need help in bearing our burdens.

February 17, 2020

A little over a year ago Barbara announced that she wanted to construct an addition to our house. We have two garages, but one of them is impossible to get into because of the angle of the driveway and the amount of space to turn. The other garage is difficult. Barbara must make a K-turn to get her Subaru into it, and my Genesis is too long and almost too wide to fit.

After investing enormous time in HGTV, she is inspired to turn the impossible garage into a combination laundry room, mud room, and play area (paint and glitter) for our grandkids and expand the length and width of the other garage to accommodate both cars. By moving the laundry room, she will be able to quadruple the size of her kitchen pantry. Additionally, since the expansion will require modifying the roof line, she is thinking that she might as well move the front door out (additional roof modification) to increase the size of the entry way (adding a whole seventy-five square feet). Even though we have a fifteen hundred square foot stone patio in the back, she seems determined to create a covered front porch (more roof work).

I love my wife. She is a perfect gift from the Lord, and I will spend the rest of my life with her. However, I question the scope and timing of her project. I have been parking my car outside for the last seven years, and the time estimate to complete this project is six to eight months. So, while my prayer would be to (finally) park my car in the new garage for several years, the smart money is taking the under.

Additionally, I eat most of the food and have never gone hungry. The likely future suggests that less food will need to be stored not more. As I carefully challenged her thought process, I foolishly exaggerated and said something like "This is going to cost $xxx,xxx," which she instantly took as a budget for the addition.

When this subject comes up while we are sharing wine with our friends, the women always remind me "If momma's not happy, nobody's happy." Men from my generation remember the twentieth century when men were men and women were grateful. Well, the men were men anyway. (Ladies please don't be offended. This is just humor for contrast. Millennial males should at least think about this before being offended.) Initially, I was pushing back on this project but finally realized she was going to do it anyway, and I might as well steal some credit for being a loving, giving, generous husband.

I think this was one of the hardest lessons for me to learn: I have influence over the circumstances and direction in my life, but I do *not* have control. In times past, usually in the middle of a heated argument, I have been accused of being controlling by my wife, children, and employees. We were taught that to be successful we needed to take control of our lives and circumstances. Unfortunately, we all eventually learn that we cannot control how people we work, live, and play with will react. We cannot control weather; we cannot control sickness and disease, and short of suicide, we cannot control when we die.

Life is easier when we accept the principle that just because we desire a specific outcome, we should not be surprised or disappointed if it doesn't happen. When you think you are in *control*, there is typically only one specific outcome that describes success. All other outcomes are a form of varying degrees of failure. By contrast, when you focus on an attitude of *influencing* a desired goal, it does not diminish the opportunity to achieve the perfect outcome and still leaves the door open for varying degrees of acceptable, improved results, or success. Lacking full control, the best outcomes we can ever hope to achieve is a result of living a life of influence.

The truth is that we all lead a life of good or bad influence. There is somebody watching what you do and what you say. To live a life of positive influence we need to be intentional. Have you thought about what it means to live a life of influence? How are you investing your influence? Are you investing in the right places? Do you need to add something meaningful or subtract something less significant so you can change your focus?

If you have been reading my posts by now, you have figured out that I value faith and a relationship with the Lord most. I chose this as the focus of my area of influence because I know how much the Lord values me and how much He values you. The God who creates and controls everything, sent His Son, Jesus Christ to earth to show us the way, die on the cross for the forgiveness of our sins, and teach us how to live a life of influence, to point others to Him.

My prayer for us today is that we will all lead lives of influence that point to our Creator and Savior.

February 20, 2020

What is your earliest childhood memory? How old were you, and what were you doing? I was five or six years old, living in Twentynine Palms, California. My father (career Marine) had given me a military issue folding shovel that I had used to dig a fox hole in the open field behind my house. I left the shovel in the fox hole overnight, and there was a flash flood that buried or carried off the shovel. I got a new shovel and my dad had me digging to try and find the original one. I started thinking about this first memory while I was with my granddaughters and grandson this past weekend.

Being a grandparent is one of the greatest experiences of my life. We spend time with our grandchildren a couple of times a week. When we are together, we laugh, tease, chase, read, eat, and rest together. When we aren't together, we FaceTime frequently. It is awesome and only eclipsed by watching our children and their spouse's tremendous parenting skills as they teach and prepare their own children with the values, direction, and attitude to be future leaders.

As I thought about my first memories, I slipped down the rabbit hole of realizing that, depending upon the growth rate of my cancer, my grandchildren might not even remember me. I started thinking, what can I do to make them remember me? Is it fair for me to continue strengthening our already tight, loving relationship, wondering if it would make it harder for them when I'm gone? What additional burden will that put on my own children? Without me, who will stop BiBi (Barbara's grandmother name) from spoiling her grandchildren beyond the already ridiculous levels they are spoiled today?

I lingered along this evil thought process far too long, feeling a little sorry for myself, before remembering (reminding myself of) God's promises, faithfulness, and the blessings that are right in front of me.

While they might not remember me, will I get to remember them? Will I get to remember the way they shout out "Boomer!" (pronounced boo-mah) when they see me? Will I get to know how I have helped positively impact their spiritual connection to their Creator and their current habit of prayer? I will never forget how I am blessed that they have great parents and won't need me to teach, coach, and protect them. I have fantastic memories in exposing them to important life skills like teasing, winning, trying new things, fashion, sharing, travel, and the importance of family.

I have been blessed that all my grandchildren live nearby, and I have already spent more time with them than my grandparents ever spent with me.

My time is in the Lord's hands, and while I am already blessed to possess so many great memories, I want to create more so that I can hold onto them throughout eternity. As I walk through this cancer experience, I continue to discover buried emotions, competing desired outcomes, and anticipation to find out what's going to happen tomorrow, to find the beauty hiding in the hope and promise of our Lord.

My prayer for all of us today is that we will not let the distractions of our circumstances interfere with discovering every blessing our Creator has prepared for us.

February 22, 2020

Last night Barbara and I caught a quick dinner and then joined a group of friends that were finishing up their dinner at a local Mexican restaurant. The place was pretty empty, but it was karaoke night. It was not long before Barbara and a few of her girlfriends had microphones in their hands and were singing, and eventually drinking tequila.

Early in my life I tried to join a few school choirs and was always invited to join some other kind of activity. I am not a singer, but I think it is great that there always seems to be someone willing to take the lead to sing, dance, speak, pray, give. God is genius in the way he fits us together (see 1 Corinthians 12:12-28), offsetting my weakness with the strength of those around me. It wasn't long before I was singing back up (no microphone).

I got into a conversation with one of our friends who had been downsized from a full-time position to a part-time consulting role. She is my age and felt pushed out at work, but also blessed, because she is dealing with elderly parents that need more help. She has been able to spend more significant quality time with them. As we talked about them, she stated the obvious, "The end is coming." Perhaps I am a little oversensitive, but I didn't hear the next few words she spoke. I looked around our table of eight with an average age in the mid-sixties and thought, "The end is coming," and I am probably the leader.

Some of you are probably thinking that Mike was feeling sorry for himself by thinking about how out of this group of friends he is going to likely be the first to die and that they will follow sometime in the maybe not too distant future. Perhaps it was the alcohol beginning to kick in, but I felt no sadness at all. In fact, I felt a sense of responsibility. That in the same way Barbara and Donna led our group out of our comfort zone to sing and embrace the moment, perhaps the Lord is calling me to help my generation of friends get more comfortable and prepared for the inevitable conclusion.

That is what I thought last night as I made a few notes in my phone about our conversation, but this morning I am having second thoughts; THIS IS NOT THE END! I need to finish this post and this earthly season of life. At worst it is the end of the beginning. Dinner does not end after the appetizer. We've already read the menu and know what is coming for dessert and the real meat of life (tofu for you vegetarians) is in the entree which doesn't fully start until the end of the beginning, when we get to live in the presence of our Creator.

My prayer for all of us today is that we don't spend so much time and effort devouring the appetizers of this earthly season that we overlook and don't leave room to fully appreciate the entree and dessert. That we don't miss our seat at the Great Banquet (Luke 14:15-24) that has been prepared for us.

February 24, 2020

Football for me was a gift from God. Wherever we moved I had an instant connection with a bunch of guys. It was something that I was good at, and it ultimately led me to a full scholarship at Duke, a school that had infinitely more value to me than just getting a degree. While the football players, for the most part, were there to get stronger, faster, and smarter to win games, the other students, for the most part, were there to be doctors, lawyers, accountants, engineers, and investment bankers. Growing up, outside of meeting doctors in the emergency room and exams for football, I don't recall ever knowing any of my friend's parents who were doctors, lawyers, accountants or investment bankers. At Duke my mind was opened to possibilities, and for the first time I became aware of money and privilege (more on privilege soon). Who doesn't want more money and privilege? Football was the key that exposed me to this much larger playing field and being a starter and team captain also expanded my previously lame social life. Football was a blessing.

Of course, with good things many times there are unintended consequences. This past Sunday morning I stumbled to the bathroom at 3:37 a.m. As I crawled back into bed, I couldn't get comfortable. Maybe it was the high humidity or the cold front passing through, but my neck was unusually stiff. Barbara has trained me to sleep face down to reduce and muffle my snoring with my pillow. I couldn't find the right angle, and this was further complicated by pain in my right shoulder. It had been separated three times and the technique of propping it up with another pillow was not working. It was 4:02, and I turned to my side (away from Barbara) to find a position that worked. The sideways torque on my knee (which had been through two surgeries) must have pinched a nerve. I got up to walk it off (a football term) for a few minutes and then returned to bed. When I slipped back into bed, I decided to pray for my brothers and sisters who are going through trials like me. Like the disciples in the garden with Jesus (Luke 22:45-46), praying late at night typically helps me sleep.

I finished praying and started thinking, if I can't sleep now what will it be like down the road when I am likely to really be struggling. Will I need to turn to drugs to manage the pain and sleep? Will that diminish my awareness and mental capacity? With the drugs will I have to give up my car and freedom? Am I about to become a burden on the people I love?

Why do we think this way? When I went to bed, everything was fantastic and then five hours later (four of which were spent sleeping), my life is virtually over. I eventually caught myself. I know that every day is a gift and yesterday was exceptional, from the morning church service till our children and grandchildren left to go home at 8:30 p.m. Today is going to be spectacular, as the Lord has already prepared a good work for me (and Barbara) to be part of. I look with anticipation to tomorrow, if it comes.

Lord my prayer today is that You will help us look past the temporary pains and suffering we are experiencing today and focus on Your promises for tomorrow. Remind us again (and again) of the depth of Your love for us, Your gift of grace and mercy at the cross, and the eternal beauty of the home You have already prepared for us.

February 25, 2020

A few weeks ago, we learned that C's mother had failed the vision part of her driving test. Previously I posted about some of the challenges of mentoring. You start with a goal to help the child but ultimately end up mentoring the family. Though C's mom is the sole breadwinner and needs to be able to get to work. Barbara jumped in to help her, and they started visiting with doctors and some local social health organizations. We discovered that she has cataracts in both eyes (she actually has three in one eye). This past Sunday we also discovered that she had continued to drive and hit a curb so hard it destroyed the wheel, and we learned that C (who doesn't have a license) had driven her to church on the donut wheel intended for temporary usage.

I love C's mom. I admire many things about her. She carries an unimaginable burden and has played from behind her whole life. I know it is born out of desperation to survive one more day, but it is frustrating to watch her make poor choice after poor choice. Free surgery to repair her eyes is available in sixty to ninety days but waiting that long to get her driver's license will be a huge burden. Her sight has been deteriorating for years. If she had taken care of it last year she could have continued to drive and work while waiting for the surgery. Now she has the additional financial burden to replace the wheel and tire. She took a job as a school cafeteria worker, which means she will need to find work for the summer. She needs more help than Barbara and I are qualified to give, which adds to our frustration.

Have you ever found yourself in a hopeless situation and wondered, "How did I get here? What am I supposed to do next to fix this train wreck?" I found myself asking the Lord (again), do I have the wrong attitude? Am I unable to visualize the solution to her problem due to lack of imagination? Am I suffering from white, male privilege? I prayed, "Lord what do you want from us?" As I prayed, I felt the Holy Spirit reminding me that the only privilege I suffer from is the privilege of suffering for our Lord. There is no greater privilege (Romans 5:3,4).

We have all heard the expression, be careful what you ask. Well, as I prayed, I felt the Holy Spirit tugging at my heart, instructing us to see it thru, to continue to stand with and support C and his mom. Yesterday I drove her to Ft. Worth for a pre-op eye exam, and Wednesday Barbara will drive her for surgery (at our expense) on her worst eye, which should enable her to pass her driver's test. Then she can drive herself to the free surgery on her other eye in a few months.

Lord, my prayer today, for all of us, is that we will not confuse suffering with purpose, that we will not let hardship, disappointment, and frustration separate us from the work you have prepared for us.

February 29, 2020

This morning I am participating in a ribbon cutting for the Oakbrook Townhome community in my city. I was introduced to them almost five years ago when I ran for city council, and they shared some significant infrastructure needs that had existed for several years. the solution was beyond their capacity to resolve without help from the city. It was clear that without help, their declining property values would continue to fall, and a very nice housing community would deteriorate. This became my first real campaign promise. I committed to helping them within the limits of city government. (At the time, I really had no understanding or experience and didn't know those before me had failed.) And now, the plumbing is repaired and the roads have been renovated. It is a great example of a private-public partnership where all sides win.

Early in my service as a council member for Farmers Branch, Texas, we had a consultant come and speak at one of our retreats. Using a baseball analogy, he described the role of local public service during our term as the equivalent of moving the runner from first base to second base. The goal is not to get to home base because the closer you get achieving your objectives, the further away home base moves.

Life is like that. The more we get the more we want. The closer we get to our initial desires in life, the more we desire. I was very content when I got my first efficiency apartment. Then I wanted a bigger one, one with a better pool. Then I wanted a condo and then a house and then a bigger house and then a second house in the mountains. I am pretty sure the only reason we stopped is that we were running out of time and money, and still, we are planning an expensive renovation on a house that currently meets our needs more than adequately. This same mindset applies to cars, boats, guns, motorcycles, jobs, and money. Sadly, for many I have also seen this desire to move up the ladder applied to spouses.

I believe we have all been guilty, at one time or another, of inflicting pain and suffering on ourselves, a type of self-mutilation, because of this type of thinking. It is a trap that can lead us down the path of self-destruction. We have all seen this play out with other people around us, but it is difficult to self-diagnose an overzealous quest for more within ourselves. We struggle to see how and why this thinking leads us away from our Creator.

Today, I offer a baseball analogy, an over simplified view of God's plans for us. With the breath of life, we are on first base, and He wants us to work our way down the narrow path to second base, that's all. From there He does the rest of the work. He removes the chains of sin binding us to second base and moves us to third and then He brings us *home*, a home that is more grandiose than we can imagine with riches overflowing.

My prayer for us today is that we can focus on and understand the simple plan that will lead us home and not be distracted or addicted by the shiny objects of this world, cheap imitations of what God has planned for our eternity.

March 2, 2020

This past Saturday I attended the reelection kickoff event for our mayor, Robert Dye. Three years ago, when Robert ran, I judged him to be a young (mid-thirties), long-haired, inexperienced, less-than-conservative candidate who, at times, didn't know how to dress, and I strongly supported his rival. Fortunately, most of the voters in Farmers Branch, Texas, were smarter than me because Robert won and turned out to be a diamond in the rough. He followed a series of elderly, conservative mayors (all great servants), and he brought fresh, twenty-first-century ideas to a community still struggling to hold onto the past.

He was and is working with a proactive council to make significant and appropriate changes to ensure we are ready to meet the needs of future generations. His event was held at a new local craft brewery (Odd Muse) and attracted a wide range of attendees including several school board members who are also involved in driving fantastic new changes for our students. It was a different crowd for me because it was notably missing the strong conservative, politically active friends that I typically identify with at these types of events. I wondered (the beer helped) why they weren't there. Farmers Branch politics is considered a non-partisan office, there is no declaration of affiliation with any political party. Was their lack of support due to disagreement with the direction of the city? Was it perhaps just a hangover from the previous election when Robert defeated the older, historically conservative candidate that I had supported? There was free beer, you would think that alone would be enough reason to show up and listen to the current mayor's comments.

Then I started to wonder if it was me. Had I changed? I took a mental inventory of my values and the issues important to me and could identify no measurable changes in my attitudes or desired outcomes. I think it mostly comes down to what we all know: *change is hard*, and our mayor is definitely an agent of change. It is one of the things I most admire about him, even when I don't agree with one of his ideas or initiatives.

Having an attitude and approach in life that is open to change is critical if we ever hope to meet or get close to our full potential. This applies to city leaders but more importantly to the people that live there. Throughout the Bible we are instructed and reminded that we need to be transformed and that we are to share the stories (testimonies) of our transformation with others to encourage them to adjust their own attitudes and plant the seed for the blessings that come with transformation. Biblical transformation is impossible if you are unwilling to change your attitude, unwilling to put your faith in something bigger than your own personal ideas and desires. It is our personal beliefs that separate us from one another. In contrast, when we pursue a relationship with our Savior, we are drawn together in common belief. We begin to worship together. We are united in all the things that truly matter.

My prayer for all of us during this emotionally charged political season is that we will not allow ourselves to be separated by worldly desired outcomes, but instead that we would strive for a higher, holy result. That we would collectively be transformed into what the Bible describes as one body by what truly matters. We all get to choose what and whom we will follow. I pray that we will choose wisely.

March 6, 2020

In addition to being a chemo week, the past four days have been as challenging as any since learning of the return of my cancer in January of 2019. While the details of the multiple stories of the week are not mine to tell, I am comfortable sharing some of the experiences of a God-filled week. There were conflict and resolutions, confessions and repentance, faithfulness, and subsequent blessings; won and potentially lost opportunities, prayer, and directional changes; all surrounded by an absolute awareness of the presence of God working through us. These individual events overlapped and involved my family, internal and external business partners, and potential new business partners. Voices were raised in anger, many tears were shed, and bridges were burned. A situation that once seemed hopeless was transformed into a shared vision and action plan where most everybody wins, and all but one important relationship has been restored. That relationship is a prayer request for next week. It has been an emotional, gut-wrenching, soul-searching, and exhausting week, yet somehow we have emerged closer and more hopeful than ever.

Over the years my partners and our company family have consistently teased me about several sayings that I have used repeatedly: "when you sleep with dogs you wake up with fleas." "Change is our friend." "They don't understand the math." "Two can play, but only one can win." "That was a self-inflicted wound." "If it dies, it dies." "People judge you on three things: how you look, what you say, and how you say it."

The message behind most of these sayings did not come into play or apply to this week's series of events, but one of the partners wise sayings summed up an important takeaway for the week: "In the long run, people will not remember your words, but they will remember how you *make them feel*." This is a reality that is so easy for us to forget. Why do we *feel* the need to demonstrate, many times unintentionally, that we are smarter than someone else, that we are in charge, that our ideas are better, and that we have the power in our relationship at the expense of people that we claim to care about. When we do this, the message we communicate is, "you're stupid," "your ideas don't matter," "I own you," "I don't respect you." I truly believe that no partner, employer, family member, organization, or friend intends to make others feel this way, but we to do it all the time. Right now, many of you are thinking "this doesn't apply to me, I would never do that." But the culture is so focused on everyone's *right* to express their opinion/position/judgment on platforms like YouTube, Facebook, Twitter without consideration (or perhaps caring) how others might feel about what you write or say. Oftentimes we are likely not even aware of our impact on others, including people that are important to us.

This journey with cancer has prompted (I tried to think of another word that was not so upbeat and more closely reflected my attitude) me to examine what is important to me during this final season of my earthly life, and it all boils down to 3 Fs: *Faith* in God, *Family*, and *Friends*. I am going to focus more on making the people that are important to me *feel* loved and affirmed vs imposing my will or authority. I would like to invite all of you to adopt the same mindset, a commitment to show the people we love and care about that they are valued by us by the way we make them *feel*.

Lord, I pray that we will be sensitive to the words and attitude with which we approach the people You put in our path. Lord, help us to share the Love You share with us, the knowledge and feeling of acceptance, the confidence that we are all important and valued by You, that they might feel what I feel in and through you: complete acceptance.

March 9, 2020

Let me start by apologizing if anyone finds this post offensive. Please read to the end before casting any stones.

The next four weeks, March Madness, is my favorite time of the year. For me it started in 1964 (I was ten) when my dad was a season ticket holder for the Wichita State Shocker, and they went to the sweet sixteen, followed by a Final Four appearance in 1965. I got to attend most home games, and for away games I would listen to the radio and keep the individual player stats on a score sheet. Fast-forward to attending Duke, and I was hooked. I have attended eleven different Final Fours. To me it is one of the purist events in sports. Following the conference tourneys, sixty-eight teams are selected for the Big Dance and get seeded. Each team's record is wiped clean. They get to start again with a clean slate. It's a "do or die" format where after sixty-four games, four teams get to go to basketball's heaven.

Here comes the blasphemy. This weekend as I thought about the tourney structure, I realized that it was a great metaphor for our individual quests for heaven. We live this season of life preparing ourselves to reach our goals. We practice, study, work with others and strive to be our best, but along the way, we all stumble and fail, sometimes miserably. Though we may feel good about ourselves, what we have accomplished, believing that we are doing better than others around us, certain of our seeding in heaven, the truth is none of us have an unblemished record. The Road to the Final Four is not unlike Matthew 7:14: "But small is the gate and narrow the road that leads to life, only a few find it."

Yesterday, I discussed this analogy between the Final Four and the Christian walk with my wife; she was not a fan. But as we talked, we stumbled on the revelation that with God, the decision, the judgment, who will enter heaven or not is black and white, and like the basketball tournament there will be winners and losers. This led to a discussion about the way we live our lives, that we don't want to see our own decisions as black or white, that we are often comfortable living in the gray areas of life, or as the Bible warns in Revelation 3:16 about being lukewarm. This is a dangerous place for us to live, and there are a few things that Barbara and I need to talk about.

Fortunately, like basketball, even when we fail, we get another chance. With focus and intention, we can still prepare better. There is always next year, until there's not. I need to be clear that I am not suggesting there is any equivalency between God and basketball, yet I know many people who are more passionate about their basketball (or other sports) team than they are about their faith. I also don't want to falsely suggest that you can work your way into heaven. God's gift of grace is what saves you, not anything you do, and once you are saved, the faithful life requires sacrifice to love others.

My prayer for all during the mayhem of March is that your team will give you a reason to be passionate, sorry Heels, and that your greatest passion is focused on your Lord and Savior.

Go Devils!

March 15, 2020

So much has happened since I posted last Monday about my love for March Madness and all the things that surround it. How could they do that to me? They replaced March Madness with a new type of madness which is going to be the topic of my post today, because nobody has heard enough opinions about the coronavirus. Being a member of the group most at risk in the group of those most at risk (cancer, chemo, platelet count of fifty thirteen days ago before chemo, sixty-six years old) I think I have a nuanced perspective based upon what I am reading online. Barbara and I were in Park City this past week watching America voluntarily shut itself down, and like most Americans we could not believe what we were seeing.

We all know that the genie is out of the bottle, and the Center for Disease Control projects, even with the actions taken so far, that as many as 160-214 million people (roughly 50 to 65 percent of the US population) will acquire the virus over a period that could last up to one year (*NY Times*). Do we intend to shut down everything for the next six to twelve months and keep a distance of at least six feet from the people we love? I cannot hug my grandchildren from that distance, and given I'm projected to have only fifteen more months, I am uncertain about the quality of life toward the end. I am determined to live every remaining day, which are gifts from God, to the fullest despite these decisions, which are out of my control and will basically leave me chained to my house watching Hallmark and HGTV reruns with my wife for most of the rest of my life. My family will not be happy with my attitude, but for me that is not living, and I would rather take my chances (carrying antibacterial wipes and washing my hands frequently) in the fantastic fray of humanity. I am not alone; many other members of the at risk group have similar feelings.

There is a new human desire to carve out a "safe space" where nothing can harm you. I learned long ago that that if we are going to embrace the life God intended for us, there is no such place. You can't ski without taking a chance you will break your leg. You can't build a skyscraper without someone walking a steel beam hundreds of feet in the air, and you can't walk outside without a chance of catching the flu.

There was a time when American men (and women) volunteered to go to war knowing that they might have to run across beach into machine gun fire or some other God forsaken place knowing that the chance of survival makes the corona virus look about as dangerous as riding a bus to Disneyland. How did our nation lose its courage? Where are the leaders that we can rally behind? At a time when many people will begin to feel hopeless, even churches are closing their doors in favor of online services and giving.

Additionally, we are taking a real medical crisis and compounding it by creating an additional financial crisis. The unintended consequence potentially could do significant damage to most American workers. According to a 2016 GO Banking Rates survey 69 percent of Americans had $1,000 or less in savings and only 15 percent had more than $10,000 stashed away. The hourly workers that comprise the largest part of the 69 percent will be the first to lose their income stream, and many small businesses will fail, bankrupting a portion of the 15 percent. Will we be measuring the increased rates of suicide as people lose their jobs and their homes?

Finally, in a nation that is founded on Christian principals, what has happened to our faith. Who and what are we leaning into as we face this crisis? Have you thought about how you are leaning into your Savior during this trial? Perhaps this is God's way of stoking our spiritual fires. Like all of life, it is a giant mystery.

My prayer today is that I have not offended anybody by sharing my personal perspective and that our thirst for light and life will overpower our fear of death and darkness.

March 16, 2020

Call it karma or perhaps just a confirmation of my sentiment from yesterday's post but about thirty minutes after I pushed the Post button on my commentary regarding the coronavirus and our reaction to it, I received a call from our neighbors and good friends informing us that they had tested positive to the virus. We had spent the previous Sunday evening with them sharing a cocktail and a fire on our deck, and she had driven us to the airport last Tuesday. The good news is that, while they are not completely out of the woods, they are doing well quarantining at home (no hospital stay necessary). The other good news is that neither Barbara nor I have any symptoms. We will be self-quarantining for the next eight days and plan to take the time to clean out all our closets and perhaps the garage, if the weather is warm enough.

The only bad news is that they are going to delay my chemo for ten days to make certain I am past the incubation period. Barbara and

I were in the Lord's hands yesterday before we heard about our friend's misfortune, and we are in His hands today. Nothing has changed except for the fact that now there is no way for me to escape Barbara's work list, though even cleaning the garage may be more desirable than watching HGTV and the Hallmark channel. I need your prayers now more than ever!

March 17, 2020

Recently during a conversation with a good friend about the financial fallout from the coronavirus, I expressed my concerns for the low-income workers that will be most affected by all the business closings. This friend, like many of my friends, sees the world from a more compassionate angle, and we have different opinions on the government's level of responsibility in all this.

The discussion with my friend turned passionate as we discussed our strongly held views and then my friend, who is strongly opposed to any type of label, did something that we have all probably have done at some point in time. He said I was greedy. Of course, I had to defend myself. I puffed up and talked about some of the charities and church ministries that Barbara and I have supported over the years. The conversation ended poorly, and I think we both walked away with a little chip on our shoulder. I am guessing that most of you never have conversations with friends, family, or work associates that end poorly like this because you are much more mature than I am but for those of you that might have, what is the appropriate response? Do we need to just provide more information and opinions to make them see the world our way, educate them? Should we just ignore them or act like nothing happened the next time we see them? Perhaps I should trash him to our mutual friends about his name calling since they all know how generous Barbara and I are.

I decided to pray about it and not surprisingly I found a little direction. First, I realized that this topic is not worthy of interfering in our relationship. In fact, it was so insignificant in my mind that it required no forgiveness. There has probably never been a more uncertain time for most Americans. The most affluent have lost 20 to 30 percent of their retirement funds, and most Americans are just wondering how they are going to get through the next couple of months. Will they have a job? Income? Will their company still be in business at the end of this so they can start rebuilding? Will they lose their home or car? Questions that I have never really had to face.

Then, there is the issue of my greed? Could my friend be right? It is easy for me to look around and believe that I am more generous than most. I more than tithe at my church. In fact, I have been proud of my generosity. And there is pride. I believe in the biblical principle "to whom much has been given, much is expected" and have tried to follow it for the last half of my life, but this accusation caused me to reexamine my values. Am I giving exclusively for the glory of the Lord? When I encourage others to join me in supporting some ministry or just to be godly givers, am I puffing out my chest? Over the past few days I have gone from "I don't think so" to "Maybe" to "God forgive me" and back again. I feel like I can't even trust my own heart, and that is not good.

Finally, I realized that these are desperate times. People are and will be hurting. Our neighbors will be hurting. Over the next months we will see more and more people in need, and we will have a choice: give more or do the minimum. We are going to have an unparalleled opportunity to share the love of our Creator and Savior. The question we each need to explore is, what will we do with it?

Lord, I pray for mercy on the people of the world, I pray for strength and wisdom, I pray for love and forgiveness, I pray for compassionate sacrifice, and I pray for eyes to see and ears to hear. Lord, I pray for revival and transformation.

March 24, 2020

I've been off the grid for a little over a week dealing with the coronavirus. As it turns out I have picked it up and have been battling moderate symptoms for the past nine days with temps ranging from normal to 101 (only two times 100 plus) and an aggravating cough. All in all, I have been blessed that it has not hit me harder, and Barbara has had no symptoms at all. Unfortunately, we shared it with our friends when we vacationed with them in Park City the week before last, and Suzette is in the hospital with pneumonia in Atlanta. Please pray for her and her husband, Stan, who is being quarantined away from her. These are strange times, but I am encouraged by some of the discovery of data and information flowing from our leadership.

Barbara sets her alarm to take my temperature every four hours and stuff me with a series of over-the-counter remedies; she is relentless. A couple nights ago at the midnight reading, my temp popped to 101 after being normal at 4 p.m. and under 99 at 8 p.m. It was by far my highest reading, and she spontaneously burst into tears, fearing that the virus was taking hold in my chemo-cancer compromised body.

We talked about how 101 was not really that high and prayed for a lower reading in the morning. I rolled over and slept while Barbara twisted and turned, unable to sleep. Our prayers were answered. By 8 a.m. my temp was almost normal and has not been above 100 since.

My question for you is, how have you been handling the quarantine? Who are you worried about? Are you concerned about your job or perhaps your children's jobs? Will their companies survive this economic shut down? Do you have enough cash on hand to survive several months of quarantine? Do you have an at-risk parent or grandparent due to assorted health issues? Have you lost a large portion of your retirement nest egg and are wondering how long it will take to come back, if it does at all? Has your spouse recently started coughing and running a temp? The press continues to call these unparalleled times in the history of our nation. How can we manage something that we have no control over? Where do we go to find comfort and peace? Have you found it yet?

This morning I was talking with my friend and business partner, Tom, about this very subject. We both believe that this "unparalleled time" is a call for spiritual revival reminiscent of what occurred during World War II when men huddled together in troop carriers, planes, amphibious landing crafts, and foxholes praying for divine intervention. Who are you trusting, doctors and politicians? Are trusting in isolation and medicine? Is it time to reexamine your faith? Perhaps over the past few years, like many, you have drifted away from the Lord. Now is a great time to renew your faith. Maybe you never found or developed a faith in God, the good news is that God's Word says if you seek you will find. There is nothing more promising, more worth pursuing than God's promise to His believers. Or maybe you are already a committed believer, and like me you are trying to figure out how we can glorify Christ during this uncertain time.

It is a time to be bold and share our beliefs and testimonies. At a time when churches are virtually ordered closed and face to face contact forbidden, we have this timely and ability to share our experiences of faith right here on Facebook or some other social media platform. The combined power of sharing how God has transformed each of us will be compelling. We all have more time than we know what to do with, so I am inviting you to respond here or just post your personal story somewhere on your own. You will not only be helping someone else experience God's grace and hope, but it will also draw you even closer to HIM during these difficult times.

My prayer for us all today is that we will choose courage over fear, hope over doubt, truth over feelings, and unprecedented love.

March 26, 2020

Yesterday afternoon I was blindsided by my wife and oncologist. Out of nowhere and without consent, they began plotting to steal my freedom. In a matter of moments, I was hustled out of my safe space (living room) and into Barbara's car, hurtling toward Baylor Scott and White hospital where a team of enemy combatants eagerly waited to separate me from my dignity. As we rolled into the emergency bays Barbara slowed momentarily to push me out the door, leaving me with these encouraging words, "call me when you get better."

I was whisked into a holding cell, stripped down, and given the traditional backless prison uniform. Blood samples were taken from several locations, and ten-inch bamboo sticks with virtually no cotton on the tip were shoved repeatedly up my nose as they tried to break my spirit by asking my name and date of birth dozens of times. They tortured me with cold glass on my back, bombarding me with X-rays and radiation, but I would not break. Then they shipped me off to solitary. I don't know how long I will remain here, hopefully just a few days.

March 29, 2020

Yesterday, in the process of fulfilling my quarantine, I rewatched the movie *Moulin Rouge*. I must admit Nicole Kidman is one of my favorite actors, and I think it is because her body type, gracefulness, and innocence reminds me of when I met Barbara back in 1977. Some of you may be thinking this is a little bit of a stretch, that I shouldn't place Nicole on such a lofty perch, but this is the way I see it. There were two great quotes about love at the end. Christian, in writing their love story says, "a story about love, a love that will live forever" and Toulouse-Lautrec says, "The greatest thing you will ever learn is to love, and to be loved in return."

The subject of love is something I have been thinking about quite a bit lately, largely because of the love so many of you have been sharing with me and my family. We have consistently experienced your encouragement, prayer, availability, and general caring in very real ways. Thank you! I think I might have learned more about love in the past five years than I learned in the first sixty-one, not because of anything I have done, but rather because of the things you and my family have done. Over the past sixteen days (excluding two in the hospital), Barbara has set her alarm to go off every four hours to wake up and take my temperature and treat me with medicine, if needed. She makes meals that I don't feel like eating and then makes me something that works. I am very high maintenance, yet the only thing she ever complains about is my slow recovery and the way that I feel. Our children are Face Timing us daily, so I can experience relationships with my grandchildren. I know that I have told more people I love them in the past few years than in all the previous years combined. It is a blessing; you are a blessing.

But I was troubled by the line "a love that will last forever." What is forever love? How long is forever? When does forever start? Do I really know what a forever love is? Can my feeble mind comprehend it? Where will we share our forever love? Who will we share it with? I believe that there is only one true "forever love" available to us. It is the love shared with our Lord and Savior. It started at creation and will move from this world to heaven and into a future, a new earth, that will be created for us.

This morning during online "church" our pastor shared a statistic that each minute sixty-two people die without knowing the Lord, without any hope of forever love. Biblical teaching informs me that God has a specific plan for each of us that allows for our "free will" to accept or reject his eternal gift of love. God also numbers our days, knows the day and time of our death. One of the things that has helped me deal with cancer, coronavirus, and pneumonia is my belief and understanding that the time of my death is already set and knowing more information about my health will not change the date or time. Believing that, it is easy to look past my daily challenges and focus on the blessing that each additional day brings. Worry will not bring me one more day. But as I think about the sixty-two nonbelieving people that are going to die in the next minute (89,280 per day), it begs the question, what are you and I doing about it? What is our plan, or do we even care? What can we do about it.? How would you describe your effort so far on a scale of one to ten? Don't believe the voice in your head that says, "there's nothing you can do." Listen for the other voice and be bold. With God, all things are possible.

My prayer for all of us is that we will experience a revival of faith and belief, that we will experience the presence of God working through His Spirit in an undeniable way.

April 5, 2020

Barbara and I are entering our twenty-third day of quarantine, and I am happy to share that I am symptom-free, and I have had a week of steady progression on the positive side. And yet, here we are still stuck in our house for the foreseeable future, feeling like there is no way to escape. This may be the most difficult time for Americans (the world) since World War II. The enemy is coming (has come) to our neighborhood, and we are all worried. Will it pass over us, or will we become ensnared by its deadly power?

We sit fearfully in our homes, mostly clustered in our immediate family pod, wondering what is going to happen to us, our jobs, our savings, our business, our elderly (sometimes sickly) parents, our children, and grandchildren. How can we protect (save) ourselves and the people/things that are important to us? The government's solution is for us to hide in our homes, stay six feet away from each other, and wait. What else can we do? There is no back door or secret tunnel or magic formula. There appears to be no way out.

Additionally, all this focus and blame casting on this uncontrollable virus enables us to ignore and/or procrastinate many of the other issues, challenges, bad choices, and outright sin that we should have control over. These issues, left unaddressed, will not go away, even with death. So here we sit, huddled in our homes, waiting, watching, hoping, and even praying for a way out of this unmanageable condition we find ourselves in. Waiting for the government to take care of us and tell us when it is safe.

This morning as I watched our church's online service, which is in a timely series entitled No Way Out on Christ's passion for saving the lost and hopeless, I felt the Spirit instructing and challenging me in a different direction. As I listened to the story today of the criminal on the cross, who became an advocate for Jesus even in the final moments of his own life. Knowing his immediate fate and that there was no way out, he still found the way in. Instead of being focused on a way out of our human condition or circumstances, we need to be more intentional about finding the way into heaven, an eternity with our Creator and Savior.

For those of us who know the way, this story or teaching is an excellent reminder of just how simple it is to be adopted into the kingdom of heaven, and for those that are uncertain or doubtful, I ask you to stay plugged in for just another couple of paragraphs.

Luke 23 tells the story of Christ's crucifixion. The attendees were a tiny group of Jesus's followers and family, a group of supportive, weeping women whom Jesus referred to as the daughters of Jerusalem," and haters: soldiers, and Jewish religious leaders who mocked Him. Those passing by shouted (don't miss the significance of this), "Save Yourself," not understanding that Jesus did not need saving but was there to save *them*. As far as you can tell from the writing only one person was saved that day. One of the two criminals being crucified with Jesus joined in with the others mocking, "Aren't you the Messiah? Save yourself and us" (Luke 23:39). The other criminal, the one that was saved that day, said,

"Don't you fear God . . . since you are under the same sentence? We are punished justly, for we are getting what our deeds deserve. But this man has done nothing wrong." Then he said, "Jesus remember me when you come into your kingdom." Jesus answered him, "Truly I tell you, today you will be with me in paradise." (Luke 23:40-43)

A criminal in the midst of mockers, on his deathbed (cross), advocates for Jesus, confesses his sin, acknowledges that Jesus is Lord, and asks Him to remember him. Luke recorded it in six simple sentences and this criminal was the first to receive Christ's forgiveness following the cross. This criminal by his own admission deserved crucifixion He made no attempt to even defend his actions and yet all that our Savior will remember is those last six simple sentences recorded by Luke's eyewitness account.

So today are you looking for a way out or a way in? Do you or your government have the tools to save yourself or are you free enough to pursue help from your Creator. Are you going to wait and procrastinate on the troubles you face or will you start to seek a relationship with your Savior and put your past behind you.

My prayer for everyone today is that, as we enter this Easter season, we will see the power and the simplicity of the cross and Christ's sacrifice for our sin.

April 6, 2020

Yesterday I was having a dialog with a friend inquiring on how I was doing with the virus. I shared with him that I was virtually symptom-free (no temp yesterday), and before the end of April I was going to be healthy enough to get in my car and visit a drive-through restaurant. I thought about the statement after I said it and realized that driving through a fast-food place was at the top of my bucket list. How far I have fallen! I am sure that I am not alone with this feeling of being trapped. I am starting to feel like a hamster, circling the cage, looking for an exit and then realizing it is fruitless. Then I jump on my little hamster wheel and start running nowhere.

Those of you who read yesterday's post probably realize where I am headed, because today, I want to reinforce the key takeaways that crimes against God or humanity do not prevent someone from claiming Christ as their Savior. The decision to follow Him is simple. The reaction of those deciding to follow Him are consistent, and the result is eternal. The criminal on the cross I mentioned in yesterday's post was trapped in a way that we will hopefully never experience, but that does not mean that we are not ensnared in some other type of hopeless trap that steals our joy and prevents us from fully experiencing all the gifts God has prepared for us. The Bible includes many stories of people who are ensnared, and today I would like to take you to Samaria and the woman at the well. If you are not familiar with the story or it has been a while since you've read it, please stop here, grab your Bible and read John 4:1-42.

This woman from Samaria who has had five husbands and is living with a man that is not her husband goes to the town well in middle of the day. She went in the heat of the day to avoid embarrassing confrontations from the other women who would have pulled their water in the cool morning. At the well she encounters Jesus, a Jew, who asks her for a drink of water. Jews did not interact with Samaritans; it was culturally and religiously unacceptable. Jesus mentions "living water" that quenches thirst forever and gives eternal life. As she asks questions about this living water Jesus confronts her sin, asking her to get her husband and come back. She confesses that she has no husband, and Jesus reveals that He knows that and tells her she had five previous husbands and that He knows the man she is living with isn't her husband. The woman said she knows the Messiah is coming, and Jesus declares that he is the Messiah. The woman goes back to her town, shares her testimony of her encounter with Jesus, and many became believers and went to Jesus and asked him to stay with them.

Reader Digest might be impressed by this short synopsis, but there are some points that should not be missed: (1) All people are welcome into the kingdom of heaven. As we cling to the importance of our diversity in our worldly living, God recognizes everyone as His and His alone. (2) Our sin is only a barrier from heaven in our own mind; Christ has already removed them if we accept him as our Savior. (3) Like the criminal on the cross who asked Jesus to remember him understood His godly authority, the woman at the well encountered Him as the Messiah. (4) Like the criminal, the woman became an advocate for Jesus, going to town, sharing her testimony, and leading others back. (5) There were no barriers preventing her from accepting the "living water" or Christ as the Messiah; it was a simple process outlined in twenty-six of the first forty-two verses in the book of John.

What is going on in your life that keeps you up at night? What worries you or has "trapped you" from enjoying life in the fullest? What issues are you hiding from or procrastinating about, just hoping that they will go away? What protective walls have you built around yourself that might be separating you from a relationship with Jesus, from your access to living water?

Today I pray specifically for those who have not yet accepted Christ and His gift of eternal life, that they would take down their walls and just simply say, "Yes Lord, I believe in You."

2020 Mike & Barbara Bomgardner

June 2016 First Grand Father's Day – Mike with Shiloh, Dustin (son-in-law) with Sadie, Ivan (son) with Emilia, Dean (father-in-law)

2018 – Mike with his 3 Granddaughters (Shiloh, Emilia, & Sadie)

1988 – Mike & Barbara at a costume party

May 2021 – Last Family Trip (before Barbara went to Heaven), Mike & Barbara, their children (Allie, Ivan, & Charlie), spouses (Dustin & Leah) and grandchildren (Emilia, Sadie, Shiloh, Mikey)

1982 – Mike's Parents (George Ivan & Betty Jo Bomgardner),
Barbara, Mike, and Mike's first child, Allie

November 2021 – The Legend Continues, Michael Ivan Bomgardner, Michael Ivan Bomgardner Jr., Michael Ivan Bomgardner II

1980 Mark (Mike's Brother), Sherri (Mike's Sister) and Mike

1974 Duke Team Captain

May 2021 Mike Bomgardner

April 7, 2020

As a member of the Farmers Branch City Council, I have been receiving weekly updates through the state and county providing data on the progression of the COVID virus. I recently got a better-than-expected update on the spread of the virus in Dallas County showing a significant reduction in the week-over-week new cases and required hospital admittance. While it is only a small sample (one week) it is encouraging especially when combined with other data I received suggesting that this will be virtually over before the first of June.

When I shared this data with a few friends, the universal response was, "I can't wait to get back to normal." I feel mostly the same way. I can't wait to hold and play with my grandchildren, spend time with my children, and catch up on celebrating birthdays. I need to get back on my chemo routine to fight the cancer growing in my body. I miss spending time and sharing a meal or a beverage with my friends, and I miss seeing and worshiping with my church family. There will be only twelve months left in my term on council when we are released from our confinement, and there are things that I would like to finish and not leave hanging for the next council. I am determined to do better at getting into the gym for workouts in my off-chemo weeks.

Yes, getting back to the way it was opens a wonderful opportunity to hit the "restart" button and pick up where we left off before this forced break from our everyday life, but before we turn the page on this chapter, I think it is worth revisiting some of the things we have learned, and could possibly still learn, from our experience. If you are like me, the way we lived before this extended break from our everyday routine was good and at times great with intermittent periods of failure, heartache, disappointment, bad choices (often money related), procrastination about important issues, sin, struggling or inappropriate relationships, and even the feeling of separation from the Lord. When I look back at the things I would prefer not to restart, I realize that virtually all of them were self-inflicted. They were things under my control. In other words, they were a result of my failure to accept the responsibility for and take control of.

This virus will go away in the next couple of months, and before we push the restart button, it is advisable to take an inventory of all the things we don't want to and shouldn't restart. This break has provided us a unique opportunity to step back and take control and responsibility for the mistakes and disappointments of our past, to turn away from our bad choices, settle inappropriate or damaged relationships, re-dedicate our commitment to our families or jobs (old or new). We have all been given this time to consider a list of things we need to reject and turn away from, to act on what the Bible calls repentance.

From what I have learned and experienced, this process of repentance seems simple. Most of us know the things we need to change. We know what we need to change, even the things we hide. We want to change, but like New Year's resolutions, the devil (literally) is in the details and execution. It requires prayer, intentionality, someone you can confide in and who will hold you accountable and then more prayer.

My prayer for all of us today is that over the coming weeks, before we hit the restart button, we will pray and take the time to identify all the negative things in our lives that we need to abandon and put behind us as we turn and pursue all the gifts God has already prepared for us!

April 11, 2020

A couple of nights ago I built a fire in the fireplace on our patio, and Barbara and I just sat there for a couple of hours, listening to music in the background and talking, and I was sipping on some Don Julio 70, my first adult beverage in over three weeks. These are some of my favorite times, sitting, watching and poking the fire, and talking with Barbara. This is where we have some of our best open conversations, an opportunity to go deeper than just reviewing the transactions of the day and get into what we are thinking and feeling, sharing the things we worry about and hope for.

This night Barbara admitted that my dance with the coronavirus had really frightened her due to my weakened immune system and especially during the time we were completely separated while I was in the hospital. She went down the path of "What if I never saw you again" and "What would I tell our children and grandchildren"? We have been facing this cloud of death that has lingered over us for the past fifteen months due to my cancer, but on this night Barbara voiced what we both live with, that we are not yet ready to say goodbye to our earthly time together. Then we acknowledged God's sovereignty, prayed for His will to be done, and reviewed the history of all that He has done for us and the way He has always taken care of us and our family. It was a bittersweet conversation with a few tears, hugs, and kisses.

Then Barbara asked me how I was doing, and I know that I surprised her by my answer. Truth be told, I surprised myself a little. I told her I felt really close to the Lord and that I have never been more aligned with His purpose and will for me than I was that night, than I am now. I hadn't really thought about this revelation of the condition of the alignment of my heart with the Lord; it just came out of my mouth. Barbara pushed for more understanding and as we talked. I recognized that there were two things influencing my relationship with our Creator.

First the process of writing these posts has changed me. It sometimes takes hours for me to capture what I am thinking and what the Holy Spirit is teaching me about this transitional and transformative time in my life. As I write I am in a quiet place. It is a type of meditation that has allowed me to more thoroughly explore my heart, the center of my good and evil thoughts and actions. It has helped me understand myself more deeply and has prepared me to accept God's purpose for my life more fully. Exclusive of a number of what Barbara might call "teaching moments" to repair my flawed thinking, this has been the most enlightening experience I can remember.

Second, over the past fifteen months I have experienced God's overwhelming love in the form of His creation: *you*. You have surrounded me with daily prayer and encouragement. Additionally, I have spent significantly more time in prayer than any other time since I submitted my life to serve my Creator. This season of prayer started fifteen months ago but moved to another level when I started writing these posts last December as I learned about so many other friends who are struggling with cancer, other life-threatening medical conditions, and a wide range of other life challenges. As I have expanded my prayer list, I find myself spending even more time in God's presence, an activity of faith that has pulled me closer than ever to Him. As I get closer, the more aligned I become with my Savior, the easier it is to see and experience peace and joy that is promised to each of us as we submit to His ways.

This Easter Sunday my prayer for us is that we will view the crucifixion and resurrection of Jesus as the proof of His love, the demonstration of His authority (over death), and His guarantee, promise, of the paradise that is available to us. I pray that we would all seek greater alignment with our Savior by expanding our prayer life.

He has risen.

April 13, 2020

Shortly after I graduated from Duke and moved to Dallas in 1975, I started playing rugby and joined a team called Our Gang, not the top team in the area but very competitive. I loved playing Rugby; it was the perfect sport for me as it was a combination of running with the ball (I was a running back at Duke) and tackling (I was a high school all-American linebacker). Our team traveled throughout Texas and into Oklahoma and Louisiana for tournaments, even winning a few sevens events. Rugy sevens are a modified, faster-paced tournament in which each side has seven players instead of fifteen.

Rugby teams are closer than many sports teams because it is basically a requirement that following the match both teams go to the home team's bar where they drink, sing, and tell stories. When people found out I played college football, they would always start in on how rugby was so much more physical than football and that football players were wimpy because they wore pads and helmets. They were always surprised, and would argue with me, when I told them that there was no comparison. Football was way more physical than rugby.

While they had never played college football, they were adamant that I was mistaken. I shared with them the details of my football experience. I would shuffle like an old man to the training room on Sunday morning for injury treatment and a long sauna before shuffling back to my room. I reminded them that we had rugby tournaments where we played up to six games (more in sevens tourneys) and that there was no way I could have played a second football game on Sunday. I asked them to consider how many players are carried off during a football game and despite playing a shorter season, the season ending injuries for a football team far exceeded a rugby team. I invited them to find just one player of both college football and rugby that had a different experience, and they never produced one.

What I have learned over time is that generally people are reluctant to change their beliefs regardless of the evidence—even if it is overwhelming.

Sadly, I must admit that over the past six months I have transformed from completely shunning Facebook to secretly snooping through my friends posts to find out what they are doing or believing. I am not at all happy with this transformation. It seems completely counterproductive to who I want to be and what I want to accomplish in this last stage of my life. This Easter weekend as I scanned through my Facebook home page, I saw several discussions on the credibility of Jesus and the cross and the belief that there is only one true God. Most of my Facebook friends have lived half or more of their lives and have already established their beliefs. Regardless of which position you identify with on this subject, unless your life is perfect, I think there is wisdom in taking time to consider and reconsider what could make your life more complete.

I grew up without any relationship with the Lord. My parents taught me that religion is for weak people. It was easy because I saw so many "Christians" spewing hatred instead of demonstrating love, judging instead of inviting, and basically saying one thing while doing another. When I was younger my life seemed hollow, so, I did what strong people do. I went to work and fought my way up the food chain. By the accepted standards I was virtually invincible. I had a big house (heavily mortgaged), fancy car (big payments, high mileage), beautiful family (I still don't fully understand why Barbara didn't leave me in the late eighties), and co-owned my own successful business. I was moving to buy my partner out (pressure of $400,000-plus-per-month payroll), which would mean taking on $690,000 in additional debt. Barbara and I took multiple extravagant vacations annually (no savings). I thought I was winning. Then in late 1991, I met my Savior, and everything changed. I turned into one of those hypocritical Christians trying to learn how to show love not hate, to stop judging and start forgiving, and to start doing what I said I would. I learned that my parents were right about religion, that I was weak and that I needed a Savior. While I have many friends on Facebook that did not know me between the ages of nineteen and thirty-nine, those that did know that I am forever a changed man through Christ. Interestingly one of my close relatives says that he can see how it has changed *me*, but *he* is OK and doesn't need to change.

If you are like me, you know many friends that have been changed and are being changed through their relationship with Christ. You've seen the positive effect on their behavior as their faith continually challenges them to be more Christlike. They slowly become better husbands, fathers, employees, and bosses. They have eternal hope, which helps them manage their fears, struggles, and disappointments in life. And when you talk to them, virtually all say that their life is better with Christ. Like rugby and football, I have been on both sides of the relationship with the Creator and can vouch for it.

My question for you is this: if you have not yet examined a relationship with your creator, will you be like the rugby player who has never played football but is certain anyway that rugby is more physical despite strong evidence demonstrating the opposite? Or will you give the Creator a shot so you can know for certain?

My prayer today for each of us is that we will recognize that we can all do better and be better, that we would have hearts that are passionate about becoming the best version of ourselves, that we would consider the possibilities and chose our path wisely, and that we would choose to pursue Christ.

April 18, 2020

Our first reaction when something goes wrong to always look back and dwell on the circumstances. Why did this happen? Why did it happen to me? If you think about it, we never have that response when something goes well. I have never heard anyone ask, why did I get that promotion or raise? Or healthy grandchild? Generally, we expect our lives to always improve and get better. After all, don't we deserve it? And yet we are always surprised when we receive bad news from a doctor or boss or spouse (sometimes the same) or bank or school. And our first reaction is to ask Why? Who are we asking? Christian or not we are directing this question to God.

Christians turn to God as if we are surprised that He would put something difficult or seemingly impossible in our path despite His consistent teaching (see John 16:33, Mathew 26:11, John 12:8; Deuteronomy 28:14, Deuteronomy 28:40, Jeremiah 15:5). We are surprised, as if we are sinless and without any fault. At times, we act like we have no hope, as if this is the final chapter of our lives. I think of Job, his faithfulness, his suffering, and his loss (children, possessions, health). Yet he remained faithful and trusting, and his life was fully restored. Why do we as Christians question our Lord's actions? Who are we to question?

At the same time, I have talked with many not-yet Christians who use suffering, loss, and hardships as the reason for rejecting Him. They blame God and reject His existence simultaneously. Why would God take my child, job, or spouse away? Why would God allow the coronavirus or cancer?

I won't pretend to fully understand God's plan for us, but I do know if all our prayers were answered and no one ever died, we would all have a much more desperate prayer. I also know that God's Word teaches and demonstrates that He uses pain, suffering, and loss to draw nonbelievers to Him. He uses Christians as an example to show others how they can find peace and comfort in impossible situations by leaning into the hope and promise that Christ revealed some 2000 years ago. For the wandering and not-yet Christians, God uses suffering to call you home to His heavenly kingdom.

This brings me to the point of today's rambling. Instead of asking *why* during our darkest circumstances, we need to start asking *what*. Lord, what are you trying to tell or show me as I go through this season of pain? What do you want me to learn? What should I do next to help comfort and strengthen the people around me who also are suffering? What actions do I need to take now and in the future to get through the season of trials? What is separating me from You, Lord, keeping me from the prize (1 Corinthians 9:24, Philippians 3:14)?

Romans 8:18 says, "I consider that our present sufferings are not worth comparing with the glory that will be revealed in us.

My prayer for all of us who are suffering will start looking forward and focus on *what* is next for us, what will get us back on the path that leads to paradise and help us refrain from looking over our shoulders to try and identify the reasons for and relive the disappointments and loss. When we're looking back it hard to stay on the right path.

Lord, keep us on the right path.

April 23, 2020

This morning Barbara and I busted out for a two-plus-mile walk, my first real exercise in about six weeks. I could tell that my quarantine, my sitting around the house watching HGTV and the Hallmark channel, has atrophied my body and especially my leg strength. Our hope is to be back in Colorado early this summer, and I need to be able to hike two-plus miles up the mountain if I plan to keep up with my wife and friends. I don't think I could do that today, and I am guessing some of you might have fallen into this same quarantine trap of sitting more and exercising less. I am determined today to start doing something about it, I just hope I have the same commitment next week when the new *Property Brothers* shows come on.

For many of us, this sedimentary lifestyle is yet another unintended consequence of the China virus. Webster defines *pandemic* as "occurring over a wide geographic area and typically affecting an exceptionally high proportion of the population." Is being weak and out of shape possibly the start of our next pandemic? Like all of us, I have spent way too much time dwelling on the virus and our country's (world's) initial response while my beliefs and faith tell me that I should be considering and thinking about how God wants us to respond. What message is He sending? Are we looking for it? Will we find it? If you have read this far you should not be surprised that I have some thoughts on this topic, and I am going to apologize again up front, because, though it is not my intent, I am likely to step on a few toes, including some that are very close and important to me. If I offend any of you, please don't take it personally and know that if I fail to encourage anyone to think about the ideas that follow, then I will have once again missed the mark.

By now we all know that this aggressive virus is easily transferred from person to person and while symptoms range wildly from none to death, statistics clearly show that the primary influencer on the severity experience is the general health of those infected. Of course, this is not limited to just the virus, our general health influences the impact on our bodies for all kinds of other diseases. Our respiratory health, blood flow, heart condition, liver function, weight, and general body strength all influence our body's ability to fight off disease. Over most of the past twenty-five of so years my weight has yo-yoed back and forth between 230 pounds (obese) and 265 pounds (really obese). Additionally, I was entertaining customers several nights a week with rich foods accompanied by fine alcohol. There is little doubt in my mind that this lifestyle affected my body's ability to fight off my cancer. If, like me, you believe God draws His people closer to Himself through trials and struggles, or even if you are uncertain, I ask you to consider the following:

God describes our bodies as "temples of the Holy Spirit" (1 Corinthians 6:19) and that each of us should learn to control our bodies in a way that is holy and honorable (1 Thessalonians 4:4) so that we might offer our bodies "as a living sacrifice, holy and pleasing to God-this is your true and proper worship (Romans 12:1). Have you recently spent any time thinking about your body as a holy temple, housing the Holy Spirit? What does treating your body like a holy temple even mean to you? What do you think it means to your Creator? Do you think you treat your body like a temple? Do you think God does?

In 2016 70 million people were considered obese and another 99 million were considered overweight. We are the twelfth most overweight country (out of 192) in the world behind a bunch of tiny islands and Kuwait. Obesity kills 2.4 million people in the US annually and smoking kills another 480,000, not to mention abuse of drugs and alcohol. As stated above I'm not the one to be calling out anyone regarding their lifestyle choices, but I do wonder if God has been calling me out. I believe He has. Do you think it might be possible that He is calling you out?

Lord, my prayer today is that we will take this time of rest (quarantine) to slow down and listen for Your voice. Please use Your Sprit to lead us in Your ways, to give us wisdom. Your word instructs us to treat our bodies like Your Holy temple. Please help us to understand what that means and give us the strength and courage to change when You call out to us. Help us to be obedient.

May 3, 2020

This has been a good week for the Bomgardners. Monday I was declared virus-free and was able to resume chemo after an eight-week delay. On Tuesday we got to celebrate our twin granddaughters' birthdays, and since we are virus-free, I got to hold and hug them for the first time in almost three months, and they got to hug us. It was a great night, and the grand girls made out extremely well as Barbara overcompensated for the three months of separation by bringing three times as many gifts as her already typical over-the-top gifting. I don't complain too much because she shares the credit (virtually all hers), and I get to contribute with what I think is important and reasonable.

We have another birthday party scheduled for Saturday, a pool party and BBQ at our kid's house. Starting to feel normal. I also resumed the chemo yesterday, and my blood has bounced back nicely. I had a platelet count of seventy-four, which is the third highest in the past fourteen months. This is the second part of the week where I am starting to feel normal. I need to go back to war against the cancer—scans scheduled for May 12.

Texas is permitting restaurants to open back up beginning tomorrow with strict enforcement of 25 percent of capacity, distancing, face masks except while eating. This is perfect timing for Mother's Day and Barbara's birthday. May 11).

It has also been a great week for our country related to the virus. Regardless of which side of the fence you straddle regarding reopening, the message is clear, we are bringing this disease under control. In Dallas County the numbers show a steady five-week decline in new hospital admissions from 185 down to 78, and ICU admissions are declining steadily from 62 to 24. This is great news, especially when you consider that testing is more readily available than it was five weeks ago (almost twice as many tests given in Dallas County from the beginning of that five-week period).

The truth is that nobody is certain what will happen as states begin to open. Will the virus begin to rapidly expand, hold its own, or continue its decrease? This concern strikes more fear in the elderly and immune compromised people (mostly over forty). The latest Dallas County statistics show that 80 percent of the deaths occurred in those over sixty-five. No one knows for certain if the lost jobs will be replaced. No one knows how quickly the economy will recover or even how many times you can watch reruns of *Property Brothers*. We started a drinking game here to spice up the Chip and Joanna Gaines reruns, drinking every time they use the term *shiplap*. Watch and drink on Zoom with your friends. While none of us really know for certain what the future holds, you can count on the fact that one of the thousands of scenarios reported online, in the press, by CDC, politicians, WHO, will be correct. Whoever is lucky enough to guess right will be an instant genius. This uncertainty strikes fear in the hearts of many and probably most of us.

Having survived the dreaded virus with my weakened immune system, I recognize that I might only have a short window to get outside. Previously I have written about how my faith has virtually removed my fear of cancer—I still have moments—and how Barbara's faith in the Lord has helped to sustain her. Dealing, or trying to deal with our fear sometimes falls short and is easily (maybe not always easily) traced back to my lack of faith. It is mostly my faith combined with trust in Christ's promises that pulls me through. This morning one of my partners shared a short Bible verse in 2 Corinthians 1:3-4 about how Jesus is the Father of compassion and the God of all comfort. Has there ever been a time in our when we individually and collectively needed more compassion or more comfort in this time of trouble? This Bible verse was not just targeted for what we individually receive from God's comfort and compassion, but this verse is primarily targeted at what *we* are to *do* with these gifts, beginning in verse 4: "[Christ] who comforts us in all our troubles, so that we can comfort those in any trouble with the comfort we ourselves receive from God." The message is clear, we are to take the teaching experiences of our comfort with the compassion we received and go comfort others, demonstrating God's compassion to them. I know there are a great number of you out there already responding to this teaching.

Father, we praise You and thank You for comfort and compassion along with all Your other gifts You so richly bestow on us. Help us in this time of despair. Help us to recognize that You love us and receive these gifts and blessings You offer us. Help us to show compassion universally, not just for people that think and act like we want them to, but even to those who have opposite beliefs. Help us to have eyes to see the people around us that need comfort (a comfort that You gave us first) and then the courage to turn around and help supply that comfort. Please give us words of Your truth that we can share with them as You teach in the verse above about comfort and compassion. For those who have been reluctant to step out in faith, we ask for the courage in our desire to be obedient. Amen.

May 4, 2020

In the spring of 1979, about this time of the year, one of my Duke soft-ball teammates had met a girl and invited her to come to a late game in the season. She showed up with a girlfriend, and he asked if I would be his wingman for a beer or two so he could get to know her. At this time, I had been married to Barbara for less than six months, and I knew the right answer. When I got home a little after midnight, I proudly told her about the beers and shared that nothing approaching immoral had taken place after the game, which was the truth. The consequence of my decision was to insert a major lack of trust into our relationship. Of course, this wasn't the first trust issue in our relationship. While we were dating there were other events that raised some questions.

Broken trust takes on many forms and feeds many emotions. When someone takes something that is yours, tells a secret that you confided or a lie that hurts you, abuses the love you have given, fails to honor a commitment, or abandons you at a time of need, it can make you feel angry, hurt, alone, trapped, or maybe even desperate. Of all the emotions brought on by broken trust, however, fear is the greatest by-product. How will I ever recover? Is he/she going to leave me? How can I pay the rent, my bills? What will people say? Does anyone love me? I need help. Who can I depend on? You don't have to think that hard to realize that it is virtually impossible to get through life without having someone you can trust, someone to encourage you, lead you, and calm your fear.

This is one of the key issues driving our fear around the virus. Our government has taken on the role of savior, asking us to believe what it says, do what it commands, and it will lead you out of this historic pandemic. Of course, our politicians are on firm ground because history shows we will certainly get through this. About one hundred years ago we made it through the Spanish Flu, which was estimated to have killed more than 50 million people worldwide (675,000 in the US).

The uncertainty (lack of trust), as I see it, is that the math changes just about every day and has swung wildly at times. There have been literally hundreds of doctors, medical organizations, university research groups, government agencies, political groups, and politicians making different forecasts. I have *no clue* as to which, if any, are trustworthy. I have an opinion, but my confidence is honestly under 50 percent, and if your confidence is higher, you are way too trusting of yourself and whichever predictor you are following. Again, the root cause of our fear is a lack of trust. Where can we find a trustworthy source that can calm our fears and restore peace into our lives?

I have found only one source that calms my fear and restores my peace, our Creator. In God's Word the word *trust* appears more than 160 times in some form. It teaches about where you can find it and where not to look. It informs on the benefits of having and understanding what true trust is versus the emptiness of looking for it in the wrong places, the places we typically look first. If you are feeling fearful and uncertain, look up Bible verses on trust and take just a few minutes to see how powerful God's Word is. It brings me peace and comfort, and I predict you will also find peace and comfort. I have listed several below.

You will keep in perfect peace those whose minds are
steadfast because they trust in you. (Isaiah 26:3)
Some trust in Chariots and some trust in horses (army/
government), but we trust in the name of the LORD our
God. (Psalms 20:7)
Why should I fear when evil days come, when wicked
deceivers surround me~those who trust in their wealth
and boast of their great riches? (Psalms 49:5-6)
In God I trust and am not afraid. What can man do to
me? (Psalms 56:11)

Lord, You do not make us to be fearful people but rather to be
strong and courageous. Lord, I pray that we will turn to You for peace
and comfort in our circumstances and that we will place our trust in
You. Help us to be an encouragement for others as we deal with the
struggles of this virus, and when we find others struggling help us to
point them to You. Lord, we praise You for all you have done for us.

May 5, 2020

Last Sunday I wrote about trust, who we trust, breaking trust, and the
consequences of lost trust, which feed the emotion of fear. Typically,
the people we trust are the ones closest to us: family and friends. Several
weeks before I shared my thoughts about the best question to ask in a
time of strife, not Why, Lord, does this happen to me? but rather, Here
I am, Lord, what do You want me to learn? We already really know why

we experience hardships. We are human. God even warned us throughout the Bible that we would face many struggles, and trust is one of His favorite topics. Many, if not most of us, are already in relationships with people marred by mistrust. What can we to do to restore broken trust?

My own significant personal experience has taught me the overriding principal needs to start and end with truth. Fast talking excuses and half- truths at best lead to only a temporary truce, and typically they deepen the mistrust. If you are ever going to regain trust, you must come clean and, as painful as it may be on the front side, share as much as the offended party wants to know. If the relationship is important to you (even if it is not), once the truth is out there, you need to ask for forgiveness as often and for as long as it takes. For complete restoration it is important for both parties to fully forgive and be fully forgiven. Next, you must change your behavior and stop doing the distrustful actions that got you into your situation.

On more than one occasion I have been a slow learner and continued to repeat stupid decisions that always lead me back to the same place. It's harder to ask the judge for forgiveness when you continue to repeat the crime. The same goes for trust. In other words, to successfully overcome broken trust, you must be committed to restoration. You must tell them how and why their relationship is so important to you; you have to tell them and show them that you are going to focus on making it better.

Now, sit back for a minute and think about your broken relationships? What did they do to you? What did you do to them? What did you do to each other? Does it matter? If they were to suddenly die next month without resolution, do you care? If you were to suddenly die next month, how many broken relationships would you leave behind? These are some of the questions I have been considering and addressing with the uncertainty of the aggressiveness of my cancer. I have successfully been working on my list for more than a year now. I still have a few to address, and I need to work harder to protect and strengthen all my current trustful relationships.

As I thought about this issue of losing and restoring trust and started to piece together ideas that might be interesting or informative, I realized that our human plan for restoring broken trust plagiarizes the simple plan for man to restore his/her broken relationship with God that is presented in the Bible. When we sin, we are, in effect, breaking trust with God. It creates the same kind of spiritual divide between us and God as our deeds of mistrust create between our family and friends.

Are you currently connected to God, or do you feel a separation? Creating or restoring a relationship with our Creator is easier than re-building trust with a loved one, but you use basically the same formula:

1) Confess, come clean, be truthful about the decisions and experiences in your life that are inconsistent with His teachings and His design for us.

2) Ask Christ for forgiveness for your sins

3) Change your actions—repent. Commit yourself to stop sinning.

4) Commit yourself to a trusting relationship with the God of creation.

5) Testify to your commitment through baptism.

I wrote that creating and restoring a relationship with God was easier than resolving those with friends and family. The reason I can say that is that your sins have already been forgiven and God wants nothing more than to be in a strong, trusting, personal relationship with each one of us. He sent his one and only son, Jesus Christ, to pay the price to remove our sin and restore our relationship, to die on a wooden cross.

My relationship with Christ is the most truthful, trustworthy, and loving relationship I have ever personally shared. I am just one of a multitude of people throughout the world who have been eternally blessed to be part of God's family. Have you ever experienced a relationship with your Lord? What is holding you back?

Lord, I praise You and thank You that You want to be in a trusting relationship with us. We thank You for sending Jesus to eliminate the barriers of sin that separate us from You. Humble us, Lord. Please give us wisdom to confess our sin to You, seek Your forgiveness, repent and turn away from our sinful nature, and commit to place our trust and faith in You.

May 8, 2020

In May of 1984 (plus or minus a year or two) I was trying to identify an appropriate gift for Barbara's birthday (May 11). We had just moved into a new home, and I had heard Barbara complain about our eclectic hand-me-down collection of pots and pans. I foolishly thought that gifting her a set of upscale cooking equipment would be a fantastic gift only to discover that she really desired something more romantic: jewelry and flowers. Certainly, I am not the first man to be perplexed by his wife's thought process, but, understanding the consequences, I took them back and accommodated her wish list.

The first six to eight, maybe twelve, years of marriage is a period of intense training and learning for men. This is when you learn that the pre-marriage courtship was just an audition to identify if you have enough potential and a teachable attitude to become the man they imagine you to be. Looking back and listening to my wife's girlfriends, apparently the selection of acceptable men that fit this "future vision" is thin.

Of course, after a few dozen years of marriage, assuming we can graduate to grasping a minimum level of retraining, you begin to comprehend the tolerable limits of give and take in your relationship. A Bible passage that helped me early on (and still does today) is Mathew 7:9-10 (I substitute the word *wife* for *son*): "Which of you, if your [wife] asks for bread, will give [her] a stone? Or if [she] asks for a fish, will give [her] a snake?" While this is a little out of context, I believe it is adaptable, and you can read the surrounding text of Mathew 7 for greater understanding. The only challenge with this verse is that it does not address what to do when she doesn't ask for something specific. She expects me to know, though I must acknowledge that after forty-one-plus years of marriage, we have mellowed quite a bit.

As I have shared in previous posts, I serve on the city council of Farmers Branch, and to support our local restaurants we have started a Zoom video series entitled "Cooking with the Council" where councilmen are paired off with the owner of a local restaurant, and we cook one of their signature dishes together online from our own kitchens. Wednesday, I joined Maggie Garcia, the owner of Nuevo León, our cities oldest Mexican food restaurant, to make chicken mole verde. Prior to recording I had cut and organized all the ingredients, connected and mic checked with everyone on the Zoom meeting, and per instruction started preheating my pan. Allison Cook, our city's director of economic development, introduced us and led us through a series of questions and answers about the restaurant and the owner's history, the challenges of quarantine, and a little about my background.

Then it was time to cook, and per the instruction I poured olive oil into the pan which had been heating up during our Q&A. Unfortunately, the pan had overheated, and as I poured in the oil the pan burst into flames. We were recording a kitchen fire. I gathered myself, collected the lid from the cabinet, and smothered the fire. The pan filled up with smoke and as I foolishly lifted the lid, the pan burst into flames again. I covered it, set it out of the picture frame, retrieved another pan, and everything went smoothly from there. Maggie got me through the recipe. I tasted the mole verde on camera (it was awesome) and toasted Nuevo León with some Don Julio 70. I am publicly challenging the other councilmen and woman to create a more interesting video experience.

My dilemma is this. The fire destroyed the first pan which was already part of our updated rag tag collection of pots and pans. Barbara's birthday is next week. I know she would really love some new pots and pans, but I keep thinking about what happened over thirty-five years ago. Surely, we have matured and grown to a point where giving her a quality gift that she could use every day (even if she chooses to use it infrequently) would warm her heart. And while she still wants to be romanced, a quality set of pots and pans is not a snake or a stone. I see it as a gift of love. It would be giving her something she wants, and something she arguably needs. Even if I have misjudged the nature of the growth in our relationship and she is offended, perhaps she will consider the fact that I am suffering with cancer and forgive me. There, I have decided. I'm heading out to the jewelry store now.

Today I am praying for all the sons and daughters looking for a Mother's Day gift, that you will give something that expresses your love and gratitude for your moms. And I pray for all you moms who have and continue to pour your heart into your children. I pray that you experience the appreciation and recognition you deserve. May God bless you all.

May 19, 2020

On May 12 I had a new PET scan to monitor the progress of my cancer. They say that trouble comes in threes, and I had just survived Mother's Day (May 10), Barbara's birthday (May 11), and now I just had to get through this scan to have a "mostly" clean slate from this trinity of fear and potential disaster. The scan was going to be telling because I had missed nine consecutive weeks of chemo when I contracted the virus, and the results would further establish a trend line for the cancer's growth. Barbara, our children, and I were all aware that the results would impact what we would be able to plan and do between now and Christmas as we have begun living in three- to six-month increments. It's funny how the unknown creates fear inside of us, and it seems like the melodrama peaks as you get closer to learning the ultimate result. There are more questions about what is unknown, and the questions come closer together. Fear breeds fear. Even people of strong faith and courage can be drawn into fear when surrounded by fearful people focusing on the worst that could happen. I think we are all experiencing some of that as we struggle through this virus season and the uncertainty about how long it will last and wondering if the people we love will be infected. Fear is not just a by-product of the unknown, it is also magnified by our own personal life experiences.

Last Wednesday I got my results, and I was encouraged by them. The good news is that the cancer in my lymph nodes and the five spots in my lungs grew a combined total of 4 millimeters, but the growth was all in the two largest spots in my lungs that grew from 9 mm to 11 mm. My doctor did not use the word *unremarkable*.

As I have shared before I feel normal and asked my doctor how large they would have to be to start making me feel less normal. She shared that she had patients with a five-*centimeter* growth that were still functioning normally and that the impact depends on the location of the growth.

I am a numbers guy and started thinking about all the different ways I could plot the trend of my lifeline. Fortunately, I did not run down this rabbit hole and only stuck my head in for a little peek because the rabbit hole does not lead me to where I want to go. I do not want to fearfully spend my remaining time fighting, striving, and denying what is unknown when there is very little unknown. I have a very good idea about how and when my Creator will bring me home. I may not know the exact time, but I know how my story ends. In fact, we all know. If you really stop and think about it, there is very little mystery in how it will end here on earth for all of us.

> "Do not fear those who kill the body but cannot kill the soul. Rather, fear Him who can destroy both soul and body in hell." (Mathew 10:28 NKJV)
>
> "Do not be anxious about anything, but in every situation, by prayer and petition, with thanksgiving, present your requests to God. And the peace of God, which transcends all understanding, will guard your hearts and your minds in Christ Jesus." (Philippians 4:6-7)

I have learned that the way for me to overcome worry is to put my faith in Someone (God) that exceeds my fear of something, anything, everything.

Lord, my prayer for us today is that when we start worrying and becoming fearful that we will remember who You are and that Tour love for us is all encompassing. While You never promised that life on earth would be easy and without struggles, pain, hardships, and loss You did promise that we could choose eternal life with You void of pain and sorrow. Lord, help us to choose well.

May 24, 2020

During my thirties and forties when people would ask me how I was doing, my standard answer was, "I have no problems that could not be corrected with more time and more money." We probably all think that life would be easier with a deeper bank account. And we probably all experience lives so full of family, work, and play that it seems like there is really no time to relax or dabble in something new that seems interesting.

For some unexplainable reason this concept of time has become a topic that I've been thinking about. It has become a more precious commodity as it becomes more finite, and like all things of value, I don't want to misuse or waste it. (Netflix is not helping; it is the devil's tool.) Virtually every day I try to think back and evaluate what I had accomplished that day, and I have to admit that most days I am an underachiever. My accomplishments are unremarkable.

Sometimes I feel like I am caught in an Eagle's song as time keeps on slipping. As I start thinking how each missed opportunity (day) is unrecoverable, I promise myself that tomorrow I am going to do better, be more impactful. I feel like Paul in Romans 7:19 not doing the good that I want. (I am no Paul.)

Do you ever feel like this, knowing that you are living a life that is nowhere close to matching your potential? Do you ever stop and wonder why you didn't do more yesterday, last week, or last month to make a difference in the people and the circumstance around you? Why did I invest the time to watch five seasons of Downton Abby last week instead of, well, instead of just about anything? Clearly, I do not have the answer about using my time, but I do know where it is.

King Solomon wrote:

> There is a time for everything and a season for every activity under the heavens: a time to be born, die, to plant and a time to uproot, a time to kill and a time to heal, a time to tear down and a time to build, a time to weep and a time to laugh, a time to mourn and a time to dance, a time to scatter stones and a time to gather them, a time to embrace and a time to refrain from embracing, a time to search and a time to give up, a time to keep and a time to throw away, a time to tear and a time to mend, a time to be silent and a time to speak, a time to love and a time to hate, a time for war and a time for peace. (Ecclesiastes 3:1-8)

And then in vs. 11 "He has made everything beautiful in its time. He has also set eternity in the human heart."

There is the answer. Is eternity set in your heart? It is in mine, and I pray it is in yours. If you are uncertain about your belief in eternal life, I am betting that there is someone close to you that has already approached you about this hope that can be yours. If not reach out to someone at your local church.

"I write these things to you who believe in the name of the Son of God so that you may know that you have eternal life" (1 John 5:13).

Lord, I pray that everyone that reads this post will seek information about your Son and come to believe in Him.

❧ ❧ ❧

June 4, 2020

Back in the early 2000s our virtually perfect son took a wrong turn down a dark lonely highway and was unable to find an exit for several years. It was a difficult time for our family as we really didn't know what to do and nothing we tried seemed to work. Our daughter, who had previously found herself on a similar dark road five years earlier but found the exit quickly, was extremely, and perhaps rightly, critical of us, saying that we were not doing enough to "save" him. We were the ones that were supposed to protect him. During that time, whenever we were together (she was already out and on her own), she emphatically and sometimes tearfully let us know that we had been much harder on her and were unjustly letting him off the hook. If she could have gathered her friends, she would have placed them in our yard shouting "No Justice, No Peace" until we came down on him harder.

Nothing will allow us to unsee the injustice of the murder of George Floyd and along with everyone else I condemn the actions of the police officer that took his life. I believe that they will rightfully face justice, both here and when they face their Creator. I pray for justice. This week as I watched the broadcasts of the marcher's and looter's shouting "No Justice, No Peace" and thought about the circumstances that brought us to this point. Despite my belief and experience that bigotry has been improving with every new generation, injustice continues to flourish and is spreading faster than a fire in a dry forest.

In the past week we have seen arrested looters released without any justice for the store owners and virtually everybody whose insurance costs are certain to rise. We saw Rod Rosenstein, the former deputy attorney general, reveal that he did not take the time to read a request by the FBI seeking to spy on an American citizen (a presidential staff member), which had seventeen false statements including an email altered to mean the opposite of the original intent. When asked how this could happen at the FBI, he said it was "inexplicable." Our last four presidents have flat out lied to the American people about important issues and supported unconscionable acts by their staff, to say nothing of our current president and his opponent. Leaders in Congress have no trouble avoiding the truth with the most extreme example being the repeated statements of undeniable proof of presidential Russian collusion to impeach a sitting president. Hundreds of congressmen have been bailed out of charges of abuse and other illegal activities in secret at taxpayer expense.

I could go on and on. No party or government organization is without blame, and yet no one is held accountable. *There is no justice in America*, at least not at the top. We all know that the values of any organization start at the top and work their way down.

Here is the good news. We can still have peace without justice. Peace is not a feeling or emotion; it is a gift. "Peace, I leave with you; my peace, I give you" (John 14:27). Christ gave peace to us and expects us to share His gift with others. "Blessed are the peacemakers, for they will be called children of God" (Matthew 5:9). We have a choice to share our peace or not. "The mind governed by the Spirit is life and peace" (Romans 8:6).

Rev. Martin Luther King Jr. was right about not judging people by their color but rather by the content of their character. What is the character of our leaders?

Lord, I pray for peace in this void of justice and leaders with character. Father, help Your children to be peacemakers, to choose peace over conflict. We pray for leaders with character, leaders that will help us seek and restore justice. Our country is headed down a dark lonely highway, help us to find the exit that leads to You.

≈ ≈ ≈

June 16, 2020

Last Saturday night we had a sleepover with our four-year-old twin granddaughters, while my daughter and her husband celebrated his birthday. While they were playing with cups and bowls in the tub, Sadie offered Barbara an opportunity to purchase a cup of pretend lemonade for forty-five dollars. My first thought was that someday Sadie is going to be a great merchant, selling advertising space at a premium price. Barbara responded saying that forty-five dollars was too much and offered one dollar instead. Sadie was determined not to accept a lowball price for her pretend lemonade and countered with two dollars. It was a fantastic example of how our minds develop. I was very proud of Barbara for showing real growth and pushing back against the highly marked-up lemonade and countering with a more appropriate price. As for Sadie, she showed real promise in countering with a less highly marked-up price. At this rate she might be ready for an internship at our company the summer after she completes kindergarten.

We all learn how to negotiate almost as soon as we are born. Before they can even talk, babies first learn to barter, understanding that when they cry, they get fed. From there it is naps for snacks, schoolwork for grades, soccer goals for cheers, work for money, cleaning your room for girlfriends. If you think about it, virtually all our life has been some sort of negotiation, and we have traded something (heart, work, dreams, pride, values, fun) for most of the things that we have or hold dear.

Experience has taught me that the people who seem to do best in the world, regardless of how you measure it, are the best negotiators. If your yardstick for measuring success is wealth, except for inheritance, successful people generally trade some combination of hard work, studious educational habits, spontaneous fun, disciplined control of emotions, and often sacrifice close personal relationships to achieve their goals. By contrast people that struggle financially often have some habit that finds them swimming upstream, against the current. The gifts they trade are anger or jealousy. They may believe they are smart enough that they don't need to continually educate themselves, or that their spontaneous nature may conflict with the need to work hard and be dependable. God gives us free will, and we are all human, but swimming against the current is exhausting.

Perhaps your measure of success is how happy and joyful you are. While happiness and wealth are not mutually exclusive, it appears to me that the happiest people are the ones that invest in other people. They place the highest values on their relationships with family and friends. The things they negotiate with and trade are their trust. They are dependable, available, thoughtful, and giving. Being right is not as important as being a friend.

There is a stark contrast between earth and heaven. While earth is a place focused on and driven by all types of negotiations, there is only one negotiation relevant to God's kingdom. He wants only one thing in exchange for eternal life in heaven. He wants us to submit to his authority. Submitting includes believing and trusting in Jesus as your Savior, confessing your sins, and for the remainder of your time here on earth, turning toward Jesus and away from your sin. Finally, it means sharing your submission with others through baptism. God doesn't want or need anything else from us.

Lord, I pray for wisdom for all of us, that we would understand the gifts and talents that You have provided for us to use and trade to carry us through our brief time here on earth, but more important, I pray that we will not miss our only opportunity to fully comprehend the incredible eternal promise You have offered in exchange for placing our trust in and submission to You.

June 29, 2020

Last week, like many, I wrote something about my dad and when I had completed it, I handed it over to my editor (Barbara) for review. Somehow, she highlighted everything, and when she handed my tablet back, I must have hit delete and lost everything. Being the mature man that I am, I had to pout for a little while before recreating my thoughts.

My father was a career Marine starting at the very bottom at twenty-two and working his way up to the rank of major when he retired. He was fighting in Korea when I was born, and his career moved us frequently and often took him away from his family. He served in Okinawa, Japan, for thirteen months while I overlapped second and third grades and left for Vietnam the summer before my freshman year of high school. During the five years in between, he served as the inspector-instructor for the reserve unit in Wichita. This required him to be away one weekend per month and for several weeks of training every year. During that time, he also had the heavy-hearted responsibility of knocking on the doors of parents to inform them that their child had been killed or wounded. Additionally, he found the time to finish his last three years of college and get his degree in math and PE. He also helped raise my brother, two sisters, and me.

His plate was full and yet he always had time for me. He coached me in football, basketball, and baseball, but most of all he coached me in life. Looking back, I know there were times when he was physically somewhere else, but I remember him as always being present and involved. He (and my mom) sacrificed over and over to keep me in athletic equipment, pay for sports travel, provide tutors to help me read better, and help me with homework or whatever I needed. He loved me unconditionally, win or lose. If I acted respectful or disrespectful, if I made him proud or disappointed him, regardless, he always had his arms open and was ready to give me a loving smile. That is not to say that I was never disciplined. I have felt the sting of a belt, switch, paddle, bare hand, and tennis shoe, but I was never disciplined unfairly or without cause. I know and believe that he always disciplined out of love and intended to help me be a better version of myself. I also know that I was given much more grace than discipline and deserved far more discipline than I received. Everything he did for me was inspired by love to make me a better man.

The relationship with my father mirrors the way I feel about my heavenly Father. During the first thirty-eight years of my life, I rejected God, believing that I could and was doing everything on my own strength, but now I can look back and see God's hand in almost every good thing that I experienced before I even knew that He knew me. He put strong men of faith all around me that encouraged me to pursue a life defined by faith. I received talents and abilities that I did little or nothing to earn. Doors and relationships opened to me without asking and "manna" always seemed to be following or leading me. I have received enormous amounts of grace and forgiveness as I have prayed and confessed my sins to Him. But, like my earthly father, I have been disciplined from time to time for my bad choices, and I have learned that when I am struggling I need to look for the lesson my Father is trying to teach me. The lesson is simple:

> "For God so loved the world that he gave his one and only Son, that whoever believes in him shall not perish but have eternal life." (John 3:16)
>
> "Love the Lord your God with all your heart and with all your soul and with all your mind. . . . Love your neighbor as yourself." (Mathew 22:37, 39)
>
> "Come to me, all you who are weary and burdened, and I will give you rest." (Mathew 11:28)

Father, we thank You for Your love, the generous gifts You have shared with us, the discipline that we so desperately need, the forgiveness you extended through Your Son before our creation, and the eternal grace You extend when we put our trust in You.

July 12, 2020

I just returned from a two-week vacation in Breckenridge, spending the last week with two of my kids, their spouses, our daughters-in-law and our three four-year-old granddaughters. It was awesome as we got to share in their new experiences, mountain hiking and white-water rafting. It reminded me of our first ski trip with our son Ivan. He was just shy of three years old, but you had to be three to attend ski school. Several weeks before our trip I started teaching him how to respond when people asked him how old he was, telling him to say he was three by showing three fingers. I was a young dad teaching my young, impressionable son, and my family, that it was okay to lie, if you had a good enough reason.

The truth is most of us are taught by our parents or friends that it is okay to lie if you have a good reason. The problem is with our definition of a good reason. Many of us, like our parents, taught our children about anger, disobedience, gossip, judgment, and unforgiveness. We don't usually teach them intentionally in the way we would teach them math or history. They just watch and imitate our actions.

I've stated previously that I want to finish well, honoring my God and Savior. As I pray about and think about what that might mean for me, what changes or actions I should take, I realize that I have treated much of my sin casually, giving too much weight to God's grace and not enough to God's judgment. I've been blessed with many opportunities for leadership and while I have been surrounded by other leaders that often hold me accountable or question my actions, I still wonder how many blessings I might have missed due to my sinful actions. It's sad that we can often identify the casualties of sin in the people around us but struggle to see it in ourselves. At work, in our families, at church, we see how the inappropriate actions (sin) of a single person can negatively affect/infect an entire organization. We have a responsibility to address sin starting with our own and confronting (in love) those we are leading. Hate the sin, love the sinner. When sin is discovered, God honors quick, decisive action, starting with prayer of repentance.

With the objective of finishing well, I have been exploring the questions: Who am I leading? and Where am I leading them? I believe these are questions we should all be exploring. Our God does not expect perfection, but He does expect to be our priority.

My prayer for us today is that we will take the time to reevaluate our sin, to remember the weight that Jesus placed on our sin and the cost that led Him to the cross to pay our debt. Please help us to always make our Lord the priority in our lives. Help us to finish well.

July 19, 2020

Last week our son Ivan and his wife, Leah, asked if Barbara and I could relieve Leah's parents on Wednesday afternoon to babysit. Barbara was not up to it, so I went alone. Our children married great spouses from great families, and Leah's parents decided to stay. Perhaps they were questioning my readiness. It was a great afternoon because I got to spend quality time talking with Mimo and Ditto and got focused time with my grandchildren.

We found a new game as I played with twenty-one-month-old Mike. He had recently discovered the meaning of "belly button" and was determined to pull up my oversized T-shirt (since I had lost sixty pounds) and put his finger in mine. As he moved in, I pulled the front of my shirt over his head and shoulders and then gave him a big squeeze. As I lifted my shirt, he had a big grin on his face and said, "More." In no time his grin turned into a giggle and then to full-on laughter accompanied by more cries for more. The only thing sweeter than a child's laughter is when that child is yours or one of your children's. It was a day worth living for, like so many others.

More was the first word that Ivan learned, and it is one of the first words our grandchildren learned. Without *more* it would be difficult to teach them *please*. I was around but don't remember when I learned *more*, but I expect it was one of my first words, and I know that *more* has been a centralized theme at every different stage of my life. Sometimes it was more food, more money, more success, more power, more love, more friends, more toys, more house, more car, more championships. Most recently, in addition to wanting more God, I cry out for more time and energy and more healing, encouraged by God's promise and the great days God continues to provide for us.

Soon our focus will shift again as we begin to seek more heaven and leave behind the pains and struggles of this world. But until then I've learned that there is still more work to be done here, and as the number of days remaining grows shorter, we need to work even harder to share more of God's love.

July 20, 2020

Some of you may be wondering why I have barely posted any updates and stories about my journey with cancer over the past month or so. I want to ease your hearts if you are worried that my health may have taken a turn for the worse or that I might be dealing with some other additional tragedy that was consuming my time and energy. My health remains good. I just had a scan last week and the results are mostly "unremarkable" to the point that I am preparing to travel in early 2021. The only current tragedy that confronts me is the cost and inconvenience of building the Taj Mahal of laundry rooms that is underway, which of course is not a topic that I expect or even want to receive any sympathy for. It is clearly a project that I have mismanaged from the very beginning, I have no one to blame but myself.

So where have I been? This is the question I have been asking myself as I look back at the last six weeks and wonder what I have done to change the world for the better. I find myself getting discouraged almost daily as I open Facebook and read through the hateful messages and outright lies posted there—many of them by good friends, most of whom confess Jesus as their Savior.

These are difficult times, and I am disappointed in *all* our leaders. Almost daily I find myself getting angry and wanting to respond to and correct your Facebook posts. I have even written several before deleting them, recognizing that there is *zero* benefit from posting, and I will only pour more gasoline on a fire that is already burning way out of control, including the fire that burns inside me.

Facebook posts fall under a few categories: (1) They let your friends know what you're up to: birthdays, vacations, dinners, births, marriages. This is good! (2) They let you advertise and sell things. (3) They let you promote partisan political information or misinformation. The vitriol of most of these posts do more to divide and inflame people than it does to promote wise thinking and actions. In past posts by friends, I have directly and indirectly been called un-Christian, uneducated, racist, a Nazi, uncaring, greedy, and privileged. While I do not suggest that I am anything close to perfection or am better than anyone else, even my four-year-old granddaughters understand that this is not the way to make friends and influence people. Drawing political lines on Facebook and demanding 100 percent compliance to make our country better is a flawed strategy. Partisan politics is bad! (4) There are still several people on Facebook (perhaps a *silent* majority) that promote good will by helping, encouraging, and supporting others. People who are willing to forgive trespasses against others, love their neighbor, and give to those in need. Sadly, by comparison when you examine the posts on your page there are far too few of these people actively supporting good.

My challenge to you today is to examine what you have posted in the past, tally which of these categories your posts fall in, and examine your motives (are you promoting hate or love?) honestly. Are you happy with your past posts? Do you believe your Creator will agree with your self-analysis? What changes will you make?

Lord, my prayer for today is that I and all my Facebook friends will filter our actions through Your word and through Your teaching. Help us to see any conflicts between the two and give us wisdom to deal with and change our ways when they are not congruent.

July 22, 2020

Last February a good friend shared a book with me entitled *Out of the Blue* by Greg Martha who wrote about his journey with terminal cancer. It was uplifting and inspirational. One of the things that Greg initiated was an event called Thankful Thursdays that continues today, well after his passing in June of 2017. He and his family held an open house in their home each Thursday evening. Friends and family were invited to come by and check in to see how he was doing, share a glass of wine, and pray together. None of my old friends will be shocked to learn that I intended to adopt Thankful Thursday and claim it as my own. Unfortunately, though, I have continued to think about this. My lack of discipline combined with my inability to plan, promote, invite, and commit turned my great idea into a nonevent.

Monday, I shared some of my thoughts about the pitfalls of Facebook that I and so many of my friends have struggled to escape. I was encouraged because over the past forty-eight hours, as I have been communicating with several friends representing both right and left, I have committed to rethink their recent habits and share their love and hope versus angry and vitriolic posts. It confirms that change is possible, and we can transform our attitudes and behaviors. Turning away (repenting) from confrontational anger, seeking retribution for real and perceived trespasses and meanspirited name calling calms your own spirit and brings peace. As I've written before, I believe, and God teaches us, that peace is an individual choice.

I have to confess that I do not like and seldom follow through on Facebook requests to make specific posts or reposts. I will also understand and not judge you if you completely ignore my next request, but I would like to hijack Thankful Thursday for Facebook. Wouldn't it be great if just one day per week (Thursday for UNC grads) when we open our Facebook pages they would be dominated with positive posts about someone or something you are thankful for or someone that did something extraordinary for other people. Facebook is at its very best at Mother's Day, Father's Day, and Easter as your read the remembrances of those who prepared the way for us. It is uplifting, and you must admit that generally the combined posts virtually every other day on Facebook is anything but uplifting. My journey with cancer has shown me that there is far more goodness going on in the world than evil if we just look for it. Despite all the challenges of my life my glass is more than half full. In fact, it is overflowing.

Together let's start a revolution on Facebook with Thankful Thursdays and remind people how truly blessed we are and share our spirit of goodwill to all. This will also lift your spirit as you take some time each week to stop and consider the things you are thankful for. Are you in? If so, please put the title Thankful Thursday at the top of your post. I also encourage you to reach out to your friends that are not connected to me and invite them to join in the fun.

Lord, today I pray for all of us, that we will take some time and stop to consider all the gifts and blessings You have provided for us, both now and throughout eternity. Help us to focus on You and these blessings and protect us from falling in the trap of holding onto and sharing our anger and vitriol.

Behind my Creator, my wife, and my family I am thankful for you, all of my Facebook friends that read my posts and pray for my health and encourage me. Last December I had a few hundred Facebook friends, and today I have almost eleven hundred from countries all around the world. I say this not to shine a light on me but to shine the light on you. Your prayers and comments of encouragement lift me up daily, you remind me that I am not alone. You challenge me to connect with you and that I need to remember to use each day that the Lord gives me to praise Him, that we all need to encourage each other to finish well. My journey is enriched by your participation, and I am eternally grateful for all of you. Thank you!

July 26, 2020

Saturday morning, I was with our twin granddaughters watching a cartoon of some masked, superhero animal that was saving some other cartoon characters. As we watched, Sadie turned to me and asked, "Why can't I have superpowers?"

This is a question I should have been prepared to answer completely, after all, isn't this a desire that we have all coveted at some point in our life. Haven't we all envisioned how great and important we could be if we could fly, disappear, stop a train with our bare hands, see through walls, or outrun a speeding bullet? Or maybe just be the star player of our team or the team that we want to play for. I must confess that even in high school where I had some good success, I was not satisfied. I wanted to be dominant and unstoppable. It was disappointing that in college I was relegated to blocking for the more elusive runners and running up the middle for three yards and a cloud of dust. Even more disappointing was the fallacy of the indestructibility of my body as it was repeatedly broken down.

I answered Sadie's question with, "Why do you want more superpowers when you don't even use the powers that you have?" While this is a concept I understood, I think I failed miserably trying to explain it to a four year old. I told her that superheroes use their power to help others and that there were still a lot of ways she could help others (and herself) by using the powers God had already given her. Unfortunately, while I could think of plenty of things within my power I could be doing to help others, I felt like I was reaching when I shared that she could do more to help her parents, her sister, her teachers, and her friends.

Why do we always want to be the star of our own story, desiring superpowers that will make others admire or even envy us, virtually effortlessly? We want extra powers and don't use the full powers God has already given us, abilities that we already possess that might make others admire us. Think about your own life experiences. Who do you admire and why? What abilities do they have that you don't have or can't develop? What is it that you admire about them? What is it that separates them from other people?

The people that I admire, the ones that are truly helping others have several traits. First, they have a superior attitude and focus on service for helping others. For me it is impossible to really commend anyone who is not actively helping or teaching others. Serving is a cornerstone for admiration. Second it requires real sacrifice. Giving something to help others that has little value to the giver is not that commendable, even if it may be meaningful to the receiver. By contrast someone that sacrifices much, or all (money, time, resources), separates themselves from the crowd (see Mark 12:41-44). Finally, they must surrender their desire to be the main character in their own story, instead shining God's light on those they are serving. These are "powers" that God has already given each of us, and yet many of us (all at certain times) fail to use them for the good God intended. We should also not forget the amazing superpower that God has promised for us: eternal life.

Lord, I pray that we would surrender our lives to You, that we would have a spirit of service and sacrifice to help those in need. Lord, please give us the wisdom to make You the center of our story.

July 29, 2020

Back in the early 2000s Barbara came to me and said, "Let's go to Israel with a tour group from the local Christian radio morning personality?" My initial response was, "No, I don't want to spend what little vacation time we get on going to the Holy Land. Why don't you ask Donna?" Apparently, I was predictable. She told me that she had already talked to Donna and that they were committed to going. To this day I am uncertain if I was plan A or B. About two weeks later the movie *The Bucket List* came out, and I realized that Israel was on my bucket list and changed my mind about going. It was one of the best reconsiderations I ever made. From that experience I learned that my initial instinct to new ideas usually defaulted to No.

Why do we teach our children the word *no*? Like *more* (last post) it is one of the first words babies learn and is the catalyst for teaching them *thank you*, a phrase that needs to be used more. We can all use and give more gratitude. Once they learn to use it, suddenly they start rejecting food that they appeared to love just two days before, and the respond to announcements of nap time with a resounding "No!" They don't want to sit down or hold your hand walking through a parking lot. "No! No!" Once the no's start they never stop. "No, I don't want to go there" or wear that or finish my dinner or get up or go to bed or do my homework or watch that or go to that college, and on and on.

But it doesn't stop there, it follows us right into adulthood. In fact, during my marriage to Barbara I'm pretty sure one of us has said "No!" to just about everything listed above. Except that when you get older you get to make a lot more decisions, important decisions which present additional opportunities to say no.

Many (most?) of the things and ideas we say no to we eventually come back and say yes once we have matured or obtained more information. In fact, in this world saying no is no more binding than saying yes. Like my visit to Israel, which was life changing for me, there are often blessings attached when no's turn to yeses. In Mathew 21:28-32 Jesus tells a parable about two sons whose father asked them to work in the vineyard. One son says yes but does not do the work while the other initially rejected his father's request but after consideration showed up to do what was requested. Then Jesus asks, "Which of the two did what his father wanted?" Then He puts the parable in context telling the chief priests and the elders that the tax collectors and prostitutes will enter the kingdom of God ahead of them because they would not accept Him or do what He taught while the prostitutes and tax collectors did.

In the world (at least the US) more and more people are saying no to the kingdom of God (heaven), accepting a worldview that we can do whatever we want without consequence. Perhaps it is time to take your first or one more deep dive into God's teaching. Barbara and I know that in the best-case scenario our time is short, but your time is getting shorter every day too. Perhaps some of you will even precede us in leaving this earth. It is time to prepare.

Lord, today I pray for all my brothers and sisters who so far have failed to put their trust in You and accept Your Word, promises, and gifts. Father, help them change their hearts and pursue a relationship with You.

July 30, 2020

This morning Barbara and I were up early with a recent scan in hand to drive to Houston for a consulting appointment with MD Anderson. I had already consulted with my oncologist in Dallas, and we were feeling upbeat about the results. We used the windshield time to touch base with several of our friends. I was kind of dreading making a call to a good friend that has been struggling with alcohol, but immediately after hearing him I could tell he had stopped drinking. He has been clean for four weeks. I learned that he has reorganized his circumstances and was in a good place. It improved our spirits even more.

My next call was to check in with another friend who has been battling cancer for about five years. When we talked, I could tell he was discouraged and learned that the long-term effects of the chemo was taking a toll. For the first time I heard him talk about the pain and the drugs he was taking to manage it. I also learned that there were days he was unable to get out of bed due to the pain and the drugs; he is losing strength. He is a strong Christian, and we talked about finishing well, keeping our eye on the prize (heaven), and a little about what that might mean between now and the time the Lord takes him home. He is struggling, and we prayed together on the phone. I felt mostly helpless as I looked for the words to encourage him.

As we spoke and prayed Barbara and I realized that our friends' current physical circumstances would likely become mine in the not-too-distant future, and the prayer I offered him was also for Barbara and me. During this journey I have determined to stay focused on the gifts and blessings I experience daily, blocking out the challenges, setbacks, and deterioration my body is enduring. Barreling down I-45 to Houston I started thinking about my strategy of not thinking about the hardship that is likely coming my way and concluded that denying my current and potential suffering might be demonstrating a lack of faith. Virtually all the disciples embraced their suffering as a demonstration of their faith, a confirmation that nothing would or could separate them from their Creator. It is not in my nature to complain about how bad I feel or seek any sort of pity—unless I am trying to get out of something I don't want to do. I want to be authentic, and perhaps shading some of the hard parts of my struggle is counterproductive in sharing my experience with cancer. It is certainly something for me to pray and think about.

Lord, I give thanks and praise for my friend that is overcoming his alcohol abuse. Help him to stay steadfast in his decision. I also pray for all my friends who are fighting cancer or other life-threatening disease, please bring healing, peace, and comfort to each of them. Help them to know and see that they are not alone, that You and we are with them and for them. Give us wisdom to lean into You, O Lord, and the determination to rejoice in the blessings you share with us each day.

July 30, 2020

THANKFUL THURSDAY

I would like to thank everyone who posted something you are thankful for or commented with thanks on someone else's post. For anyone who missed my post last week, I am suggesting that each Thursday we should try and flood Facebook with positive, thankful, and uplifting comments about people or things in your life, and for one day each week (Thursday for UNC grads), we can change the tone of the typical, angry, hateful, politically charged theme that sadly seems to dominate Facebook. Last week I must not have been clear as many just commented thank you instead of creating your own post.

This week I am thankful for my daughter in law and son in law.

Both of my married children have chosen outstanding life partners. They all value God, their family, their commitments and possess a strong work ethic. My son's wife, Leah, always has a mischievous smile on her face and is such a joy to be around. She can find joy in frustrating situations and always has a clever comeback if you leave yourself open. She loves our son and his family, is an excellent mother, and is generally just awesome.

My daughter's husband (Dusty or Aggie) is a foot taller than Allie. He is even keeled in high-stress situations, is a great father, provider, and saver. He is a unique blend of West Texas country values mixed with big city financial and IT skills. He is patient with our daughter and granddaughters. He is always working on a project around the house, is outstanding outdoor chef on his green egg, and leads his family well.

There is an added blessing because both couples have become great friends, raising their families less than a mile from each other, and they have demonstrated time after time that they have each other's backs during times of need. It is a huge comfort to know that if the Lord took me tomorrow, they will have the kind of great adventure Barbara and I have been blessed to share. Now we are all just waiting on Charlie to find that amazing woman that God has planned for him.

I am blessed and thankful this Thursday.

August 4, 2020

During the past three days I have been reaching out to my family members and a few of my spiritual mentors to update them on some changes in the progression of my cancer. Thursday afternoon I met with my consulting oncologist at MD Anderson in Houston. After reviewing my recent scan, the doctor found twenty small lesions in my lungs and wanted to change my medication to fight the growth. This is not what

I expected or wanted to hear, after all I feel perfectly normal when I am not taking chemo and still can't imagine that my body is failing so profoundly. If there is one thing that I learned from football is that the film doesn't lie no matter how strongly you feel that you never held that guy. Once again, my "feelings" had led me to a place of false security.

My doctor suggested a regimen of pills (twenty-one days on and seven days off) that he said is often successful in slowing the growth for around six to ten months and that it should help me maintain my quality of life during that time before moving on to something else. I shouldn't have been surprised. Twenty months ago, my oncologist said that the average life span for people with my stage of disease was about thirty months, but this is one of the few times in life I was and am expecting to bend the curve to the upside. Once again God reminded me that He is with us, preparing the way, and that as much as this "feels" like a big change, in reality, nothing has changed.

On the way down to MD Anderson I spoke with a close friend who has been fighting cancer for more than five years and is taking medication to fight his pain. He is unable some days to get out of bed and is on his fourth or fifth medication change. We are on the same narrow path that leads to our ultimate home, but it looks like he is a little ahead of me. That conversation opened our eyes and led to an intimate discussion with my wife about the inevitability of my future progression and how we might handle it together and separately. God had prepared us for what we were going to hear in just a few hours, and while it is not the news, we wanted to hear it did not rock us or steal our joy.

The good news is that while I have watched many people in the infusion room struggle with their treatments, I have had twenty months of feeling great with the promise of many more. I know harder times are coming, but I don't want to waste a single day worrying about the future. I will endure the struggle when it comes. I know when the time comes it will be a challenge, but my faith tells me, and the Bible teaches me, that it is *not* permanent.

Thank you for your continued prayers and I ask that you might pray for my family specifically, and love on them if you get the chance. This is more heartbreaking for them than it is for me.

Lord, You know that we are all going through something difficult, and while it may not be a life-threatening disease, it still causes pain, despair, sadness, and conflict. Father, I know that I keep asking for peace and comfort and strength in our lives but that is what we need. Help us to feel your calming presence as You overcome our other feelings of fear, worry, and hopelessness. Thank You for Your grace and mercy. You sustain us in our times of need.

August 5, 2020

Tomorrow is Thankful Thursday, and once again I encourage you to post something positive that you are thankful for to change the tone of Facebook for just one day per week. I thank those of you who have taken a kinder and gentler approach to your political posts. Spewing hatred is counterproductive for anyone who wants to make the world a better place.

This past week has been emotionally challenging. I have held onto and wept with more friends and family than any other period in my life. I have a great appreciation for embracing friends and loved ones whether saying hello or goodbye or I've missed you, I love you, I forgive you, or I'm sorry. We all know that sometimes we just need a healing hug, and we should never pass up the opportunity to share one with someone in need. There's been a lot of sharing going on around here.

There have also been a lot of tears, and I don't know how I missed it these past sixty-six years, but this past week I had a revelation on the importance and comforting value of tears.

My daughter and her family were out of town this past weekend and last night was our first opportunity to spend time together following the news of my cancer's new growth. When I arrived at their house, she just hugged me, and we wept together for a while. There were no words that could have comforted us, and we repeated the same exchange when we headed home. Every hug that I have shared with my sons this past week were similar: long and tearful. This week I learned what women have known for years, that tears can be more effective than words in communicating emotions of love, significance, sorrow, and hope in a relationship. They have healing power.

In Luke 7 Jesus tells the story of a sinful woman who washed His feet with her tears. Jesus described her actions as showing great love and said, "her many sins have been forgiven" (Luke 7:47). There are countless examples throughout the Bible of apostles and profits weeping, and even Jesus wept with Mary and other friends of Lazarus after learning of his friend's death (John 11:35).

Lord, sometimes we face difficult situations and lack the words or understanding to comfort people in need. Thank You for the comforting gift of tears. Help us to share this gift with the people You love when they are in need. And, Father, we look forward to Your eternal promise where tears are not needed because all pain and problems will be gone.

August 10, 2020

When my thirty-eight-year-old daughter, Allie, was in seventh or eighth grade another dad and I agreed to take our daughters and a couple of friends to and all-day music festival at the Texas Motor Speedway. To make it easier to coordinate in the morning, we had all four girls spend the night. In the morning when they came down, Allie had blue hair. While she certainly is not the first or last teenage girl to push the boundaries, she did have a special knack for some over-the-top drama, and for about two rebellious years she spent most of her time swimming against the current and making her own life more difficult. We were in the battle with her offering advice and reminding her that we were *for* her, but she could not understand that the primary reason we were trying to get her to change direction was out of our love and wanting the best for her. It took a few years, but she finally got it, and sometimes she even comes to us to ask for advice.

By comparison I was thirty-nine before I stopped trying to swim against the current. Up until then, despite having a wife and two young children, I was selfish, greedy, prideful, and sometimes undependable. And along the way I had a bunch of friends that were encouraging or at least ready and willing to follow me down virtually any dark, narrow path. This was before I understood that I also had a Father, a heavenly Father, who desires the best for me. A Father that has prepared a place for me and a Father who loves me enough to call me back or discipline me when I take the wrong path.

For some reason yesterday's sermon got me thinking about this concept of swimming against the current. The Holy Spirit revealed to me that most of you will probably wonder what took me so long. He showed me there are two major currents flowing in conflict with each other. There is the strong current of the world that appears wonderful, and it is easy to throw out your "floatation device" and just ride down the current having fun with your friends. This worldly current surprisingly ends with the most beautiful waterfall. You can hear it as you get closer to the end. At this point the smart ones instinctively start swimming against the current to escape the destruction that awaits.

And then there is the current of the river that leads to heaven. This river has a few forks that lead to somewhere else, so sometimes you must swim a little to make certain you stay in the "heart" of the main current. As you float down this river, you are surrounded by "eternal" friends, all excited by the new home that is waiting for them at the end of the river.

Which river are you on? Are you floating with the world, or have you found your way to the river that leads to heaven and spending an eternity with your Father and His family. It is never too late to change your direction, to change your destination.

Lord, I pray today for the world, for everyone that finds themselves floating in one current or another. I pray that they would see You for who You are, our Father who wants only the best for His children. For those floating with the world, I pray that You would give them wisdom and strength to turn and swim to You.

August 19, 2020

It's been a busy ten days since my last post. On August 11 our "daughter in love" had surgery to reconnect a severed tendon in her toe from a falling knife. We helped watch Emmie and baby Mike (a.k.a. Spike).

While babysitting I received all the details on our city's two-hundred-page, $140 million fiscal budget for 2021 to review and prepare for our budget retreat. On the very same day our "son in love's" Grandmother Freda Faye, who raised him along with his grandfather, coded twice. Freda was everything you would imagine from a woman that spent her entire life in West Texas and much more. We shuffled through the weekend helping wherever we could.

Monday brought morning conference calls, intense budget study, and an afternoon and evening city council meeting. Tuesday and Wednesday I had all-day budget meetings and learned midday on Tuesday that Freda had been promoted to heaven. Early Thursday I saw my oncologist who surprised me by suggesting that I take at least two more rounds of the current chemo and then another scan (there had been conversation about me moving to a pill form), so I spent much of the day in my comfortable lounge chair, until about 2:30. About 4 p.m. my brother, who lives in Colorado arrived for a three-day visit while Barbara went to DeLeon, Texas for the funeral on Friday. I forgot to mention that we had work crews at the house and no front walkway that required everyone to walk around to the back. We squeezed in as much family time as possible, and I learned that my body has a few more limits that require some rest that I didn't get.

On Monday night (last week) Barbara (BiBi) had gone over to help watch the twins while Dusty went to the hospital in Ft. Worth and prepare to remove life support. When BiBi walked in, little Sadie (four) ran up to her with a big smile on her face and announced, "Freda Faye is in the hospital and is going to die. She's going to heaven to be with Pop" (BiBi's dad who had died thirteen months ago). Her mother had a little talk with Sadie and told her that this was a sad and serious situation, and while I wasn't there, I assumed she talked about all the people that would miss Freda. Throughout the past week as I replay Sadie's words, I have come to wonder if she was the only one that got it right. After all, shouldn't heaven be our primary, perhaps only, real objective? Jesus said, "Let the little children come to me, and do not hinder them, for the kingdom of God belongs to such as these. Truly I tell you, anyone who will not receive the kingdom of God like a little child will never enter it" (Luke 18:16-17). I invite you to stop and ponder this. What does it mean to receive the kingdom "like a little child"? I believe it aligns nicely with the fruit of the Spirit: love, joy, peace, forbearance, kindness, goodness, faithfulness (Galatians 5:22).

On Friday, at the luncheon following the services and viewing, and burial, Sadie walked up and asked, "BiBi, where is Freda Faye?" No doubt she was having lunch with Pop and Jesus.

Lord, help us to see the world around us as You see it and to have the spirit of a child. Help us to see things and events in our lives with the pure wonder of Your creation. When we get lost, please help us to remember to just turn to You.

August 23, 2020

THANKFUL THURSDAY

This week there is so much to be thankful for, but I am going to focus my gratitude on my oncologist and her support team. During this cancer journey I have been blessed by so many people, more than just friends and family, that have been praying for and encouraging me, but not just for me, they also lift my family. You all are amazing and give me more strength and courage than you could ever imagine.

For the past twenty months or so, I have been visiting my oncologist, Dr. Flippo, and her team about every other week on average. Even these past months, with all the extra COVID protocols, everyone I see—receptionist, nurses, phlebotomist, schedulers—share their best attitudes in an environment filled with death and uncertainty. For one day every other week I sit in a room filled with a mixture of people of all races, genders, and ages. If you look around carefully, you can identify the hopeful, often just by the way they enter the room and chat up the nurses and search the room for a chair next to someone that doesn't look defeated. The hopeless are easy to spot. They are tired, and their body language is withdrawn, and they avoid eye contact. The most difficult to recognize are the patients in the middle, in the process of losing hope, who are sometimes angry, needy, and moody. Of course, the chemo room is not a one size fits all. It's more of a custom shop where everyone has a unique cancer diagnosis, is at a different stage of growth, is fighting with different medications, and is at different levels of faith (often a topic of discussion between me and the person sitting next to or across from me). You make friends and see people that you suddenly stop seeing and wonder and pray that they are just coming on a different day for some reason.

About once every fourteen days I experience this emotional confrontation of participating in this chemo ritual that is taking place five days a week, knowing that I do not have to endure or face the consequences of those needing radiation. By contrast every day that Dr. Flippo and her team come to work, they recommend medications that have difficult side effects to heal their patients knowing that many times the treatments will not be effective. They must cling to the blessings that accompany lives being saved and quality of life being extended.

I have been seeing Dr. Flippo and her team since early 2016. She and she alone is the one that delivers the good and bad news (though Dr. Nelson from MDA gets to pile on a little). At the end of 2016 we rejoiced that the cancer was gone. In January 2019 we wept at its return and the incurable nature of what I have. Together, every other week, we review the decline of my blood tests and make a short-term plan and review our long-term goals. We both know it is a losing battle, and yet she is still fighting with me to get another first down. I am grateful for her partnership in this likely final stage of my life, and I am thankful to her and everyone on her team.

Every Thursday I encourage you to please post something for which you are thankful and share something positive in this world to counteract the division and hate.

August 23, 2020

What are your greatest disappointments in life, the things you wanted most, the things you dreamt about but never came to be? Maybe that ship has already sailed and the window has closed. We are always quick to replace the desires of our heart with some new fancy, many times before the conclusion of our current goal. We are always hoping for something. It is what keeps us going (or at least me).

This morning at church I was reminded during the sermon that no matter how wealthy you are you can never buy the thing that is most precious; time. I've heard this sentiment hundreds of times, and I'm sure I used it more than a few times, but for some reason this morning the message resonated more deeply. Why have I been so ignorant and naive, so unprotective in the use of my time in the past?

I am not writing about time today, but these were the thoughts spinning in my head when I started thinking about hope. I can't control or even influence time, but I am the owner of my hope. I get to choose the things I hope for. I get to determine how important and valuable they really are by intentionally putting myself in position to be ready to receive whatever it is that I was hoping for. This is an important step in achieving your dreams.

I started thinking that people generally line up in one of three categories. They are hopeful, hopeless, or somewhere in the middle with momentum that is driving them to one side or the other. This has never been so clear as it is when watching the circumstance in which we currently live. So many people have an overwhelming fear that they or one of their loved ones will catch COVID and that if the other party wins the election the world as we know it will end. People are afraid that our coasts will soon be flooded with glacier melt. They think police are killing minorities and worry about how they are going to find a job or their next meal. Fear, crippling fear, is the major driver of hopelessness, and hopelessness drives anger. People are angry.

The hopeless need hope, but even if they are looking for help, they most likely don't know where to find it. Do you know where to find it? Do you know how to share the source of help? Will you share Jesus with your hopeless neighbor?

Lord, Your Word says to "fear not" 365 times, and yet at times we all struggle to hear You. Lord, I pray for those being held back by fear, that they would recognize the source of their hopelessness and begin to look for hope. Father, I also pray for all who know their personal source of hope and that we would freely and confidently share how Jesus brought hope into our own lives.

August 27, 2020

THANKFUL THURSDAY

I am very thankful for all my Facebook friends that have taken the time to write something positive about someone or something that has influenced our lives in an effort to change the tone of Facebook for just one day per week. I encourage everyone to take the time to join me in this effort.

This is my fourth Thankful Thursday post, and I realize that it is way past time to share with you how thankful I am for my wife, BiBi. I believe women change when they get their grandma name. It is a little surprising to me that she has not even dropped a hint about not feeling great even though I have noticed she has been experiencing back pain, headaches, and fatigue. I am pretty sure that if Family Feud ever had a question about excuses women use to deny their husbands these would be the top three answers. I am trying to believe that this is all just a co-incidence of age colliding with an active life and schedule.

Cancer—not unlike starting a family, children leaving for college, the empty nest, and retirement—has created an interesting change in family dynamics. Many of these new changes have been extremely rewarding for me. My kids are making more time for the family. While COVID has altered our commitment to go to church together, we have drawn closer these past four-plus years.

When I look back at this period, I realize that I have at times used my cancer and treatments as an excuse to neglect my responsibilities. I am embarrassed to say that it has gotten to the point where Barbara makes to-do lists for me, and I am surprised she has not fired me for incompetence. I know I would have. She also has taken over much of my schedule and availability. She is the one that sends our children home when she sees me getting tired while I would stay with them until I dropped. She is the one that reminds me to nap, so I get the rest my body needs to fight. Our children know that I am an eternal optimist, choosing to see everything through rose-colored glasses and focusing on God's blessings for the day. Though I have never been dishonest with them about my health, the question they ask me is "how are you feeling," and the question for Barbara is "how is he doing" because as time moves forward, she cannot afford to view the future with those rose-colored glasses.

God has blessed me through Barbara over and over—through all the dreams, trials, changes, victories, and the impact that she had in helping to lead me to Christ. She has comforted my heartbreaks, failures, and disease. She has loved me despite my selfishness, considerable time taken from her and the kids as I traveled and entertained extensively while she contributed most of the impact in raising our children.

She is not flawless, but God knew all the qualities needed to bless me through this journey called life. I love her more today than ever before and as someone that follows and respects trends, I expect I will love her even more in the days, weeks, months, and Lord willing, even years to come.

Lord, I am *thankful* for the boundless blessings you have bestowed on me through Barbara, and I pray for all husbands and wives, asking that their journey together will reap the same or even better joy and favor that we are still sharing today.

August 30, 2020

Back in early December of 2019, when I started posting about the return of my cancer, I shared that the first decision I needed to make back in January of 2019 is What do I believe? For almost twenty months now, whenever fear starts creeping in and I begin to lose my way, I remember what I believe in order to correct my thinking. But recently I have become much more aware of how, even among the most biblically based evangelical Christians (I like to think I am one), we express and share our belief very differently, often focusing on different areas of Scripture. Nowhere is this more evident than Facebook.

Over the past months I have received around two hundred friend requests from Africa and having been hacked I look through each of them to evaluate the threat. As I look through their friends and their recent posts, it is impossible not to recognize that Christ is first in their lives. They share all their upcoming church and small group events, including invitations, live video, pictures, and Scripture. Their pages shout out, "I am trying to walk with the Lord and come walk with me." They have reached out to me personally through messenger, and I get calls through messenger all the time, sometimes several a day to the point that I am embarrassed because I don't have the bandwidth to engage with them all. Since last December I have accepted more than eight hundred friend requests and utilize the same examination process to avoid hacks. Most of these are from committed Christians, but there are also many "currently undecideds" that are struggling with cancer and other medical and life adjusting issues. Many have loved ones walking through a difficult season and of course we are *all* dealing with COVID. Multiple times Jesus promised us hardship not smooth sailing.

What do you believe and how do you express it? When I read Facebook posts, I see an overwhelming effort by so many that seem more interested in promoting a presidential candidate or party with barely any evidence of effort to save "loved ones" from an eternal hell. What do you believe? Do you believe either Trump or Biden would have the authority to destroy the world, or do you believe God is in control? Are you crippled by fear worrying about what is going to happen to you or your loved ones next or do you trust God when He tells you to not be afraid and to fear not? What do you believe?

My idle time combined with my desire to meditate on ideas that are relative to my goals and purpose and avoid hard physical work have me thinking about the other important questions beyond What? If I can avoid the labor, I will share my thoughts about when I first believed to be followed by why and how.

Lord, tonight I pray for all my Facebook friends, that we would stop and really think about what we believe, what is important, and how we can share our beliefs to help others. Lord, send Your Spirit to guide us to submit to live lives that reflect You and Your priorities and not our own selfish desires. Humble us. Thank You for loving us and saving us. We praise Your name, Jesus.

September 3, 2020

THANKFUL THURSDAY

This has been yet another tough week here at the Bomgardner household. We learned late Tuesday the Barbara has stage 4 pancreatic cancer that has also invaded her liver in multiple locations. We have spent most of the week circling the wagons, loving on our children and grandchildren, calling family and a few of Barbara's close friends, praying and praising God virtually nonstop, and once again reordering some of our priorities. It has been hard.

During one of our calls yesterday someone said that you just can't prepare for this type of news. I will be the first to say that I was not ready to hear this. To a large degree I am still stunned, but I don't think that

Barbara and I are completely unprepared. For one thing we have walked down a similar path before and as I have stated previously, we know what we believe. We were already trusting in Christ, and nothing can change or separate us from our belief. We know who fights our battles. Also, we are already surrounded by a large network of family, friends, and prayer partners that support and encourage us and always have our backs. We know that we are not in this struggle alone. This week I have shed more tears clutching a friend or trying to choke out words on the phone than any previous year I can remember. It was heartbreaking to tell my children twenty months ago that my cancer had returned in a currently incurable form, but not nearly as brutal as having to inform them that their mom was cutting in front of me on the path leading to heaven, that both of us will likely be abandoning them in the not-too-distant future.

Last night as I was thinking about Thankful Thursday and what I was going to write, I had two thoughts. First, ever since I shared the concept of Thankful Thursday and encouraged others to join in to change the bitter attitudes expressed on Facebook, a little over a month ago virtually everybody in my family has endured an emotional heartbreak or physical malady or maladies. Second, while Barbara and I continue to praise and worship our Savior, I was challenged to think of something I was truly thankful for right now. Then the telephone rang and an old friend who had stepped back from his relationship with Christ two decades ago called to let me know that he had heard the news about Barbara. For the first time in twenty years he had gone to his knees to pray for her alongside his wife. Through this process I have heard from several other friends that they were also exploring and expanding their relationship with their Savior.

This week I am thankful that our Creator might use the struggles and hardships Barbara and I are facing to potentially rescue some of our unbelieving friends and hopefully family members from eternal hell. (I know that hell sounds harsh, but I couldn't think of a better way to say it.)

Father God there are so many of us struggling with hardships of every nature, caught in both physical and spiritual war. Many are battles that we cannot wage on our own. We need Your help. So, Lord we ask for help. Help us to have courage to stand with or behind You. Help us to remember that You are our Creator, Savior, and hope, and nothing is beyond Your power and authority. Help us to trust in Your plan and design for our lives and submit fully to You.

Thank you for your love, mercy, and promises.

September 4, 2020

I want to thank everyone for your birthday wishes, comments, and acknowledgements. It has been a crazy week, and I wish I had time to respond to each of you individually. Please know I cherish each of your comments. I had a great gift as Barbara was released from the hospital to come home. Thank you again, and may God bless you all.

September 5, 2020

Last Monday I wrote about what I believe is the key to navigating your way through a difficult crisis, remembering what you believe and where you put your trust. Little did I know that Barbara and I were about to be tested again (see Thursday's post). I am happy (?) to report that though this has been a very difficult week, we are unwavering in our trust and submission to our Lord Jesus. Having shared *what* we believe I want to examine the process of knowing I could confirm what I believe.

Back in the early mid-nineties, just a couple of years after I had submitted to Christ in baptism, I played in a coed indoor soccer league with a bunch of coworkers. There was a young player on the other team that was physically reckless, including knocking over some of the women. The Reader's Digest version is that I antagonized him to a point where he came after me. When he did, I wrapped him up in a form tackle and, restraining myself, set him gently on the carpet-covered concrete, nose to nose. I pinned his head with mine, borrowing a line from one of my college roommates saying, "you don't want to mess with me tonight." As we were separated, I felt a small sting on my chin. When I pulled my hand away from my chin, there was blood on it. He had bitten me. I was just a little enraged. The next day some friends were searching for his address, so I could serve a little justice. I next morning I had my weekly breakfast with my spiritual mentor, Pastor Ron. After explaining why I had stitches on my chin, Ron walked me through what the Bible (Jesus) said about vengeance. He talked me off the ledge, and then we ended up praying for my assailant. As we finished the prayer my anger was instantly gone, and I was at peace.

When you first give your life to Jesus you have no idea what you are committing too. I just knew I needed help and wanted the joy and the peace I saw in the people I met when I first started going to church, people with hard circumstances like the types we are going through. At the time I felt like I was struggling through life and virtually everything was still going my way. I had to learn things that did not always come easy, like forgiveness, loving my neighbor, learning who my neighbor was, giving, worshiping, praying, truthfulness, unselfishness. These are all things that did not always come easy or naturally. They required intentionality and prayer while I still fail frequently.

So how do you know *when* you really start believing? What is the test you can self-administer? I believe it is when you first react like Jesus to the circumstances and challenges of life rather than the way you used to respond. When our children were teenagers the test they used was, "What would mom say that Jesus would do?"

So how about you? Has your response to the challenges of life changed? Do you act and react in a Christlike way? When did you start? Now you know the *when*.

Lord, help us to see the events of our lives the way that You see them and respond the way You have shown us with love, self-control, joy, peace, patience, kindness, goodness, faithfulness, and gentleness.

September 9, 2020

Back in the spring of 2019 Barbara's dad (Dean) was really starting to struggle. He was in and out of the hospital, rehab, and had to be moved to assisted living. His mind was great, and he was a joy to talk to and even occasionally share a wee dram of very good single malt scotch. He was a great man. His mind was solid, but his body was failing him. I was doing my best to prepare Barbara for the inevitability of the not-too-distant future. During that time both of her out of town brothers were in a little bit of denial. They would look at Dean's best moments of the and assume he could get back to where he was. They were filled with hope, just as Barbara and I are now.

Dean went to be with the Lord in early July 9, 2019.

Flash forward to a conversation I had with my daughter, Allie, this past weekend. We were sharing our thoughts as we continue to get aligned with our faith, our new processes, and evaluating the changes to our future plans. These are hard conversations to have with your children, the parents of your grandchildren. In the process of sharing a few tears with her I made the comment, "Allie, let's remember that each day is a gift, and let's not miss a good day today worrying about tomorrow. Besides we are not circling the drain yet." Allie didn't hear the last part and asked me to repeat the part about circling the drain. When I did, she informed me that she thought I said, "circling the dream."

I have been dwelling on this subliminal thought and believe it is the Lord's way of correcting my view, or at least correcting the communication. As we approach the end of our time here on earth, we are not circling the drain but rather we are surrounding the ultimate dream God has prepared for us. I don't feel like either Barbara or I are in our "dream spiral" (not death) yet, but when I start circling, I am going to be seeing heaven from every angle with anticipation of seeing our Savior face to face. Feeling the excitement of my sight replacing my dream (faith).

Lord, as we venture through this earthly life You have planned for us, help us to not be distracted by earthly things, but instead, please keep us focused on hope that we have through You. Keep us on the narrow path that leads to the dream You have prepared for us.

September 10, 2020

THANKFUL THURSDAY

I continue to encourage anyone and everyone that is disappointed with the daily bitter tone on Facebook to post something each Thursday about something positive, something you are thankful for. It could be something about a relationship, an answer to prayer, a pay raise (call back to work), about someone that you admire.

Despite learning that Barbara has stage 4 pancreatic cancer and having to share that information with family and friends, I am thankful the results of the last seven days have turned out beautifully in so many ways:

1. This past week I have watched all my children pull together and lean into their faith. While our conversations were painful and emotional, their words and thought process were constructive. It demonstrated a strong bond and unity among them; it was a proud and freeing moment.

2. The calls, visitors, meals, and prayers by our church and its leadership has been an encouragement. I cannot imagine anybody feeling more loved than Barbara and me during this past week.

3. Our oncologist and team have been a blessing. Tuesday Barbara had her first office appointment with Dr. Flippo, who is the perfect combination of science and compassion. She walked us through the next steps, and we are all on the same page about extending Barbara's quality of life. Her office is a safe place in a building where war with cancer is waged.

4. I had a CT scan on my birthday. The report came back that everything (growths) remained stable and had not increased: *unremarkable*.

Despite the large number of sweet moments shared last week and the comfort and peace we received, I am also thankful that I won't have to repeat the sadness and pains felt these last seven days.

Lord, I thank You that even in the worst of storms You strengthen our faith and our bonds and send Your servants to provide everything needed to sustain us (especially love). You provide great doctors and an answer to prayer in the form of the clear scan. Lord, I pray that during times of struggle that we would have eyes to see all the gifts that arrive when the struggle begins and ears to hear the sweet voices of love and encouragement.

September 13, 2020

In late February of 1971 I returned from my last (of about ten) football recruiting visits and signed a scholarship with Duke. From a perspective I was leaving the nest and would now be flying on my own. Despite being a little naive, it is hard to explain how excited I was for this next season of my life.

In early August my parents dropped me at the Philly airport with duffle bag containing everything I owned in hand. I flew into RDU airport three days early, so I could watch the varsity team, who had already arrived, start practicing and get a lay of the land. I just knew it was going to be an amazing experience and didn't want to miss a thing.

In late February, four years later, I returned from an interview in Dallas with an offer in hand. Perhaps a little foolishly (there was nothing wrong with the college life), I couldn't wait to get out of college and onto this next season of my life. I graduated, went home to New Jersey, packed my car, and drove to Dallas. I was pumped and couldn't wait to discover the new adventures in store for me.

Both experiences included a significant element of sadness. When I went away to college, I left my family and my friends, and when I left for Dallas, I moved even further from my family, high school, and college friends. There was an unavoidable sense of loss that comes with new seasons.

Like all of you, I have experienced many changes of seasons, all filled with both anticipation and excitement coupled with loss due to the change. I think that is why it is so difficult for many to accept change because they do not want to endure the sadness of loss. I got married and had to sacrifice time with some of my friends who liked me better when I was single. Nothing has been received with more blessing and more sacrifice than becoming a father. And then you're a grandfather with a new name. Retirement was a hard new season. I missed the people I had worked with and the challenges of managing a business, but I still had spent years making a bucket list, saving money, anticipating the raw freedom of not having to set an alarm every morning. Now, the Lord appears to be rushing us through the retirement season.

I'm sharing all of this to help you understand the excitement and anticipation I am developing for the approaching season(s). Like all my previous seasons, the Lord has prepared me with the understanding and tools (faith) to make the transition when the time comes. I know this new adventure comes with more sadness and loss than any other to date. It has already been tearful and crushing, but it also comes with a promise that exceeds anything we can even imagine. And that is something to strive for, to be ready to receive, something to be hopeful for, something to look forward to more than anything we have hoped for in our lives to date. This is my current mindset.

Lord, You love us, shape us, and grow us throughout the various seasons of life, and we thank You for the way you prepare us and the way You never leave us to struggle alone. Help us to look forward with excitement and anticipation as we grow and discover Your perfect plans for us as we move through the seasons of life. Thank You for the way You love us.

September 17, 2020

THANKFUL THURSDAY

A about four and a half years ago I reported to Texas Oncology for my first round of chemo. I arrived with a mission: I was going to use every part of me to destroy the cancer. I started a diet, and as my body screamed for food, I imagined each pain being a cancer cell starving to death. When I wasn't hungry, I spent significant time in prayer and imagining the cancer cells shrinking to nothing. I could not wait to start the chemo because I knew it would destroy the cancer. As you know I am still fighting over four years later and enjoying life with our family and friends. I'm blessed daily by God.

Today was Barbara's first day of chemo. There were several significant differences with my experience and her circumstances. First, for more than two months Barbara has been suffering with the severe pain of blood clots in her legs and lungs. Second, because we were scrambling to start treatment and because of Barbara's use of blood thinners, we had to start her chemo with a pick line, which is way more uncomfortable and painful than a port. Third, she was getting more chemo than me. She takes all the chemo I do plus one additional drug. This drug will probably rob her of her beautiful, long, thick, blond, tresses over a short time. And finally, her demeanor is very different than mine. When she sees conflict, her starting point is peacemaker, while I must get past resistance, anger, pride, and repentance before I even get near peacemaker.

Barbara is home and taking a well-deserved nap, and I am so *thankful* this Thursday turned out to be a 9 or 10. I have seen her get tough, especially when there was conflict involving our children (sometimes tough with our kids), but this morning as I dropped her off, she was strong. I could see it in the way she marched into the building. As strong as she looked going into the building, she was more resilient on the way home and was already putting together a grander list of things we need to do by the end of the day tomorrow. This Thursday I am not just thankful for the test results but also for all your faithful prayers. No one can convince me they don't make a difference. I am also more than thankful for the way Barbara continues to surprise me in so many spectacular ways.

Father, we love You. We praise You and are thankful to You for the way You love, provide, forgive, cleanse, strengthen, train, and plan for our eternal future. Thank You.

September 24, 2020

PART I

For years one of my canned responses to the question of how I was doing: "I have no problems that couldn't be resolved if I had more time and more money." Perhaps you are somewhat like me and view time and money as two of the most precious resources that impact your quality of life. These are resources that we know we need to use carefully, to save for future needs, spend thoughtfully, and share with those in need. These are also commodities that we often carelessly waste for selfish purposes. We tend to treat them and talk about them like they are virtually the same, of equal importance. But are they? Should we value time and money as equals?

Looking back I realize that historically most of my past was spent more on acquiring and managing money than preserving and protecting my time. We've all heard the expression "Time is money," and I spent a disproportionate amount of my time focused on making money and getting ahead of my peers. It's funny how quickly your perspective can change with a single trip or two visiting the doctor. Where did the time go? What opportunities did I miss by saturating my life with so many mundane and frivolous activities. How should I ration what is left? What things are important enough to allocate a portion of our remaining time to? These are some of the questions that have been rattling around in my head for the past twenty-plus months and have only intensified over the past few weeks.

The answers seem to be a constantly evolving series of priorities and objectives with expanding strategies to meet the goals. For example, I have transitioned from primary care receiver to primary care giver. My main priority is taking care of Barbara. I have also replaced her as the primary communicator to family and friends of what is going on with our health. I will not be nearly as effective. We have prioritized family pictures, a trip to Disney World, and are trying to evaluate Barbara's ability and endurance to host friends both in town and from out of town. Unfortunately, the harsh reality is that time is slipping away. The days or shorter as I need more rest, and every day I get one step closer to meeting my Creator. I have this urge to create a plan to maximize my impact and memories for my children and grandchildren. I literally have almost one hundred people that I would like to find a way to spend some quality time with before my strength starts failing and take care of Barbara. I could plan for every waking minute and still come up short. How should I allocate my remaining time here on earth to get the best results?

More and more I am starting to realize that I am so busy that I am crowding out the one strategy, the single source of all my blessings. I am not making enough time for Creator. I pray daily, but I don't always prioritize the time to pray. Often, I am praying on the fly, perhaps routinely at meals, and virtually every day I read something that reminds me to pray. I pray for many of you. But as I examine my prayer habits, I have come to realize that my prayers are often superficial, and while I ask my Lord for blessings and miracles, peace, and joy, I am not crying out loud enough for my children and grandchildren to be rooted firmly into the Lord's family through every stage of their lives. I realized that I have not prayed for the future spouses of my grandchildren (and son). I talk a good game, but my actions demonstrate that my prayer life still needs an overhaul. I need to start by allocating enough time to pray deeper, to activate the Lord's power and authority to do the important things that, not being God, I have never been able to do on my own.

Father, God, we thank You for the abundant blessings You bestow on Your children. Lord, help us to spend more quality time, not just talking to You but more importantly listening for the voice of Your Holy Spirit. Teach us to make Your plans our plans. There is no one else more trustworthy than You.

September 24, 2020

PART II

THANKFUL THURSDAY

This has been our toughest week to date. Barbara's first round of chemo last week crushed her blood quality, and she has struggled to stand for more than a minute. She has low energy and no appetite. Tuesday, they gave her a blood transfusion, but she developed a recurring bloody nose and basically bled all the new blood away. Today, they tested her blood again, and the numbers were already lower than Tuesday's. It was also a chemo week for me, and in my transition from care receiver to care giver I did not stay hydrated and didn't eat enough. Fortunately, I figured it out before it got bad and got some fluids in me.

I know our battle with cancer is troubling to our friends and family, especially our children having to watch both of their parents fighting stage 4 cancer at the same time. I have been searching for ways to help them through this difficult season. Over the past months several people had suggested that I read the book *Draw the Circle: The Forty Day Prayer Challenge* by Mark Batterson. Monday night a wonderful friend handed me a bag with a note and two copies of the book suggesting that I could use them for a one-on-one, forty-day personal study together with my daughter, Allie. She has been struggling with the sadness of our circumstances and is excited that this would drive daily prayer and conversation together. We did the first of forty chapters today, and we are off and running.

Last Thursday I was thankful for the loving physical support we received from so many of our friends and family. This Thursday I am thankful for the spiritual support and encouragement—your prayers; speaking God's word to me; suggesting and purchasing books for a study on prayer so I could spend quality time helping my daughter and possibly even learn something at the same time— from so many of you.

Stay Positive!

September 27, 2020

Back in 2013 we took our final (?) step in the downsizing process and purchased a smaller home. Barbara was excited about the process because the home we purchased was virtually a blank slate. There were no floors, plumbing, lights, or electrical outlets. Barbara, with the help of her not-so-budget-minded friends got to pick everything, reasoning that since this was going to be our last house, we should build it out the way we want it. At the time I had visions of our four-year-old grandchildren in their twenties poking a little fun at our decorative choices the way we poked a little fun at the bubblegum pink floors, tile walls, bathtub, and toilet at the house Barbara grew up in when her dad moved into unassisted living a few years back. I barely balked at the sometimes-over-aggressive spending to make our house just the way she wanted it, taking solace that this last, one-time expense, would cover us for the next fifteen to twenty years.

I can't decide if I was completely foolish or just naive. Three years in I was informed that the kitchen and dining room lights she selected were no longer desirable, and it was time to do some remodeling. Shortly after we got rid of those tacky light fixtures, Barbara and her friends started a campaign to convince me that our laundry room was small, inconvenient, and unacceptable and that we needed to convert one of our garages into a laundry room where she could do more than just clean clothes. We also needed to build another garage to replace the one we were losing. These changes would require moving our front door out about twenty feet to improve the look and size of our entryway, which would require adjusting the roofline and replacing the front sidewalk and landscaping. I know what most of you are thinking. I have been married for over forty years and have lost the credibility to convince anyone that I was naive. For my wife, remodeling is a constant endeavor to continue to make our home better and more hospitable for our family and friends.

Saturday morning, I was talking and praying with Allie, and as we leaned into the Lord together, praising Him and redeclaring our trust, she made a comment about how God was "building" our character as we work through these trials together. As she said this, I had a personal revelation that God is not trying to build our character, He is remodeling it to become more like His. Even though it might feel like it, He doesn't tear us down and start over. He finds an area in our life that needs improvement and shines His light (perhaps in hard ways) so that we can see where and how we need to change. He is remodeling us to spend an eternity with Him in His kingdom. We are God's project, and in the same way Barbara wants her house to be more perfect.

Lord, this is just one more way that You show Your love for us, not just preparing a place for us but more importantly preparing us to inhabit Your place. Father, we ask for wisdom to recognize all the times You invest and shine Your light on our areas of weakness so that we can renovate our thinking to be more like Yours.

September 30, 2020

THANKFUL THURSDAY

Last Thursday I shared about the difficulty of the weeks we have endured and the blessings of so many friends that were lifting us up with physical and spiritual support. As God's ambassadors you have literally carried us through this harsh conquest in which we find ourselves engaged. I cannot thank you enough!

Since last Thursday Barbara has endured eight separate trips to our oncologist or hospital. Despite all of this, during the last five days, she has made substantial progress. In fact, this afternoon she drove herself to the hospital to get an iron infusion to hopefully enrich the bone marrow to produce more platelets and blood cells. This is the first time she has felt able to drive in over a month, and her appetite has returned. Yesterday afternoon I was the only one that needed a nap. She is not entirely out of the woods, but she is feeling good and perhaps even on her way to frisky.

God has heard our prayers and answered them. His timing is perfect as this coming Saturday we are hosting a celebration to shout out that Charlie is a Bomgardner (formally Dodson) and is fully part of our family. We have dozens of family and friends coming from out of town and will be hosting a family-only dinner on Friday night with twenty-five family members. (Those who are not able to come should not feel at all guilty and will be roasted throughout the weekend).

This Thursday we have much to celebrate, and God gets all the glory. Have a blessed weekend.

October 7, 2020

THANKFUL THURSDAY

So much to be Thankful for this past week. Saturday evening, with my wife feeling better than any day in the whole month of September, and with beautiful weather, we celebrated the adoption of our adult son, Charlie Bomgardner. It was a perfect night.

Yesterday, Barbara and I had our very first date at the chemo infusion room. Our day started at 8:45 a.m. with a blood test. Over the past twenty-one months I have developed a relationship with a vampire named Sean. From the beginning I adopted a strategy to show up to chemo wearing a Hawaiian shirt and an attitude that I am coming to sit in an elegant lounge chair while the "bar maids" (nurses) serve me cocktails. When I arrived to give blood, Sean told me that he was going home with my shirt because it would look better on him, probably a true statement. I surprised him by saying if he could get me one of their Fight Cancer T-shirts I would give him the shirt off my back. We swapped.

We then went to meet with our oncologist, who informed us that Barbara's blood had shown amazing improvement. Her platelets jumped from 47 to 448 and that the liver enzymes showed great improvement. She stated that this was consistent with new information regarding her cancer cells, which were described as mutants. Apparently, these mutants are not as good at resisting chemo as the pure cancer cells, and this gives us great hope. In fact, while we understand this is an early reading, it was perhaps the best news we have had this year.

Our doctor laid out a strategy for sixteen more chemo treatments over the next thirty-two weeks, which she believes will shrink the cancer to a level that can be maintained with pills that are less invasive. She also suggested that Barbara would likely be able to travel to Colorado in about four months. This is all very encouraging and is clearly an answer to all our prayers, yours and ours. I can't thank you all enough for your prayers and support.

This Thursday, and every Thursday, I encourage you to post something on your Facebook page that you are thankful for as we attempt to change the divisive comments and attitudes that seem to dominate Facebook every day.

≈ ≈ ≈

October 13, 2020

I watch and play with all my grandchildren, and if you are a grand-parent, you know there is no substitute for the joy and laughter their energy and ideas bring to any party. When they are present, it mostly seems like it's always a party. They are all unique in the way they think, the interests they pursue, and their personalities. Even at age four the twins, raised in the same environment, have very different strengths and weaknesses, personality traits they will carry throughout their lives.

I used to think that we develop our strengths to offset our indi-vidual weaknesses. For example, during most of my life I have been an accomplished procrastinator. Why do today what you can put off until tomorrow? I would especially put off tasks that don't hold my interest. In college I pulled all-nighters writing papers and studying for tests with copies of someone else's class notes. I only interviewed for one job com-ing out of college, accepting the first offer which moved me to Dallas. I can be a disappointing friend, often putting off reaching out to people who are important to me. I can find ways and reasons to procrastinate on almost anything, sometimes including writing these posts and even pushing off the Holy Spirit. When you are a procrastinator like me, ul-timately you have two choices: perform well under severe and at times constant pressure or fail. Despite failing a few tests, sometimes failing my friends, and starting a few businesses or investments that didn't work out, I hate failure. Learning to overcome my habit of procrastina-tion has forced me to step up and into the furnace and find a way to finish what needs to be done.

Being an overcomer is a biblical principle that comes with heaven-ly rewards. (Read the early chapters of Revelation.) Recently I have been wondering if I didn't learn it backwards. Could it be that my ability to perform well under pressure combined with my selfish sinful nature allow me to get away with procrastinating more and more. Perhaps I am not the overcomer that I think I am or want to be. Am I fooling myself into believing that I am better than I really am? Am I fooling you? I know that I cannot fool my Savior. These are questions and concepts worth considering and reconsidering.

One thing that I am certain of as I approach the end of the path is that the time I procrastinated away that could have and should have been spent with my friends and people I love will never be recovered by any pressure-filled performance. That time is lost, and it is one of the few regrets I will carry to heaven with me. Please forgive me for treating our love and friendship so carelessly. I encourage you start making a list and a plan to spend time with the ones you love.

Lord, thank You for not procrastinating with us and demonstrating Your Love for us first, some two thousand years ago, when you sent Jesus to the cross to pay for our sin. Help us to understand the depth of Your love for us so that we can demonstrate Your love to all the people that You love.

October 15, 2020

THANKFUL THURSDAY

Today, I am so thankful to share that it appears that we may be breaking our 2020 trend of repeated storm after storm. It has been three straight weeks of continued improvement for Barbara as she regains her strength from basically being bedridden for six straight weeks. Virtually every day she has more energy, needs a little less sleep, feels better, and is generally back to her original self. Additionally, as expected, this past week we purchased several wigs, and she made the transition with virtually no remorse. Her attitude is amazing. We have planned an eleven-day vacation to do the whole Disney World, Universal, and beach experience. What seemed impossible three and a half weeks ago now feels very doable.

This week we are also blessed with friends coming from Atlanta and Nashville to share their time with us. We continue to be blessed by our friends near and far showering us with prayer, encouragement, support, and food. Thank you all.

October 22, 2020

THANKFUL THURSDAY

Yesterday, I had the pleasure of having lunch with the Farmers Branch city employee's and thanking them for their service. This is an annual event that is typically catered by a local business, and the city council and city managers serve the food, but 2020 is just a different year. The food was served by a food truck, less handling and COVID friendly distancing. Yesterday was my sixth and likely last time to serve the police, fire, and city staff, the people that protect, save, and enhance the quality of life of the citizens of Farmers Branch.

I never thought about or wanted to run for city council. In fact, when I was asked to run, I said no several times, but as I was asking God what he had planned for me following my "retirement" this was the door that kept opening. I learned a while back that when God opens a door for you, even if it is not something you covet, it is always a good choice to walk through it. Serving on the city council has been a blessing and has changed my view on several fronts. I used to believe that many government workers were not as committed to excelling at their job as public workers, but my experience with the Farmers Branch staff has reminded me once again to not always trust in the things I believe. I am so thankful for the opportunity I have had to work with these passionate employees in our city. If you live here, you are blessed with the most responsive and dedicated police and fire departments. Our city services are second to none, and our fiscal condition is outstanding thanks to the leadership of our city manager and his department heads.

I am so thankful for all the great people I have met while serving and will certainly miss being part of a great team when I term out next May. Thank you all!

October 30, 2020

BELATED THANKFUL THURSDAY

This week, following more than three months of work, our home-improvement project is basically finished. All that is left are a few touch-ups and to pay the final installment. It turned out great, and I am thankful to finally put this project behind us. Yesterday, I was able to get my car in the garage for the first time since we moved in more than four years ago.

I am also thankful that this election, featuring two very disappointing presidential candidates, is almost over. It has been the most divisive election in my lifetime and has divided families and friendships. It seems that the longer it goes, the more bitter people have become. I am prayerful that the people supporting the losing candidate will concede amicably and the winners will be gracious so that we can start healing our country. Will you be part of the problem or part of the solution?

I pray that you have had much to be thankful for this week and that you are feeling God's blessings pouring out on you. Have a great week!

November 2, 2020

In one of my earliest posts, I shared details from the conversation Barbara and I had in early January of 2019 when I learned I had stage 4 colon cancer. Our bucket list shrank considerably, and we changed our focus to family legacy, eternal issues, finding quality time to spend with family and friends, and just finishing well. Given the changes in my quality of life and life expectancy, we adjusted our bucket list accordingly. We have discovered that if you want to be happy as a couple, it is important to agree on the direction you are headed. One of these areas is the bucket list. Since we adjusted our direction, we have most everything on the revised list checked off.

In other words, Barbara, giving into my dying wishes, gave up more than she took related to the content of our bucket list. One of the items that did not make the first cut was Disney World, as I logically pointed out that the girls were three and four and would remember very little from the adventure and that she could take them multiple times after I departed. I don't want this to sound wrong (which means it probably will), but Barbara has a habit of getting her way, which somehow always turns out best for me (another mystery of marriage). Not to be denied

Barbara came up with an aggressive form of cancer and asked for one thing: Disney World with the family.

The planning is furious. Allie has put together a forty-day count-down using forty rings like what we made out of construction paper for the Christmas tree as kids. Each ring has a daily tasks (watch Mary Poppins, learn and sing a Disney song to record and send to your grand-parents, open a special Disney gift, etc.) written on the inside, so they could count the number of rings left to know how long before we leave. They wear various Disney Princess dresses at some point nearly every day. The excitement and anticipation are off the charts, and it is conta-gious. Day 1 Magic Kingdom!

It would be negligent for me not to mention our twenty-eight-year-old adopted son (Charlie) who has also never had the opportunity to visit any Disney property. He holds the same magical expectation for our trip as the girls (but without the dresses).

This is the same, magical picture that the Bible paints of heaven, only the "magical" promise of heaven is even greater. Our granddaugh-ters have seen many pictures of Disney, sung the songs, and watched the movies, while heaven is described as unimaginable beauty. You must pay to go to Disney World and work to make the money to pay for it. Christ already paid for our trip to heaven, and biblically no work is required as you cannot earn your way. At Disney you eventually must go home. In heaven you are home. Yet in one very important way they are identical. The best way to enter Disney World is to have the faith of a child, and it is the same for heaven. Will you put more focus into going to heaven or visiting the Disneys of life?

Lord, give us the faith of a child! Help us to seek Your kingdom with excitement and anticipation! Jesus, we praise Your name.

November 5, 2020

THANKFUL THURSDAY

It has been another outstanding week for Barbara and me. On Monday we had our date to infuse our chemo cocktails. This day always starts with blood tests and consultations with our oncologist. While we had a minor setback—Barbara's white cell count was too low to take her chemo—we learned that her cancer marker, which had started at 5600 at the first of September, has been steadily falling to 2900 following first chemo, 2100 following the second round, and now it is at 900. Additionally, all her liver blood tests are now in the normal range. Our doctor was expecting such a result following the discovery of the "mutant" cancer that Barbara has. They gave her a shot on Monday to help with the white cell count, and on Tuesday it had recovered enough for her to receive the chemo. We both coasted through our chemo week without incident.

It seems that for weeks now our prayers have been answered, and I am eternally thankful for all your support. My cancer markers are remaining steady. Barbara has a scan scheduled near the end of November, and mine is in early December.

I pray that this next week will be outstanding for all of you and look forward to reading about the blessings in your lives and what you are thankful for. God bless you all.

November 22, 2020

It's official, we have survived eleven-days in south Florida, visiting Disney World, Universal Studio, and a long weekend at Clearwater beach. Taking on a trip of this magnitude with three four-year-old girls, a one-year-old baby, two grandparents with stage 4 cancer, and our five adult children, mostly in adjoining rooms revealed how naive we all were. We were up early to feed the kids and ourselves so that we could be at the park when it opened, and most nights we finished late, either at the park or at our hotel pools. The grand girls all started with very different confidence levels regarding which rides were acceptable. This ultimately caused a few meltdowns, though I am happy to report that by the end of the trip they all loved the scariest ride of the entire trip (Harry Potter). Coordinating meals in the parks was also challenging as we typically needed to go to several food kiosks to accommodate different tastes. This created an uneven distribution of food, which caused a few melt downs. As the week wore on everyone got progressively more tired, which led to a few more meltdowns and even some minor bickering among the adults. Our trip was mostly filled with laughter and smiles and the memory building we were hoping for, plus a few more. Our prayer is that these memories will last lifetimes.

Like any effort to accommodate the needs, desires, and whims of eleven people, there was room for improvement, and we have been talking about what we could have done to make it better for future trips. Some of our thoughts included shortening the trip, taking some days off in the middle to rest, find a teen girl to bring along as a babysitter so the adults could have a mental break and enjoy some mature conversations. Despite the great time we had, the days added up, and we seemed to progressively lose some of our peace and joy. At times moving and managing the girls and their emotions started to feel more like work than a vacation.

After being home a few days, I started to realize that BiBi and I had been so engaged with helping to get children fed and dressed to rush to the parks for most of the vacation that we had neglected our time with the Lord. It was disappointing to realize how easily I could be distracted from the source of my strength, peace, and joy. I rolled over without a fight. For almost two weeks I lost the narrow path and paid the consequences: lost peace and joy almost immediately.

Have you ever woken and suddenly realized that you are on the wrong path, a path filled with uncertainty, hardship, pain, and fear, a path absent of joy, peace, and hope? Fortunately for all of us, the Lord has provided a shortcut to find the right path. All we must do is turn around—known as repentance—and actively seek the path that leads to our Lord. God's promise says, seek and you will find. I feel like I have already made good progress as my peace and joy have already returned.

Lord, my prayer today is that all who read this, especially the people who recognize they are not on the path that leads to fulfillment, will submit, and seek Your path and Your promises.

December 2, 2020

This morning I called my good friend and business partner Tom to share some great news. Before I could speak, he accused me of butt dialing him last night. I explained to him that I had just acquired a new iPhone because my old phone would not hold a charge and was struggling to work efficiently when charged or connected to power.

I then went on and shared the news that I had just left from a meeting with our oncologist. She shared miraculous information about the results of Barbara's scan from last Wednesday. The radiologist's report indicated that the surgery appeared to be completely successful, and there was no evidence of cancer in her pancreas or liver. The *only* problem with the report is that she did not have any surgery showing that her six chemo treatments had completely shrunk the tumors. One was as large as 3.5 centimeters. She did not use the word *miraculous*, but she did say that she had never witnessed such a rapid disappearance of tumors the size of Barbara's. And she works in an office with several oncologist's and for a company that has multiple offices throughout Texas. My heart and my head can only view this as miraculous.

I also told Tom that I was getting my scan next week to which he replied, "The Lord is not finished with you." It was at that point I realized that maybe my faith was weak, and I should have chosen the phone without the button. Friends and loved ones, thank you for your faithfulness in prayer, support, and encouragement. Please continue to pray for us and specifically for my scan next week and that I will come to regret choosing a phone with yesterday's technology.

Lord, I thank You for Your mercy that You have poured out on Barbara with Your healing power. Thank You for deploying Your children to shower us with prayer and love. Help us all to be faithful to You in spite of our circumstances. To God be the Glory!

December 10, 2020

THANKFUL THURSDAY

While we continue to soak in the miracle of Barbara's recovery (confirmed this week by our oncologists' own words), the past week has been entirely full of joy. This past Friday, Saturday, and Sunday I picked up my three four- year-old granddaughters for one-on-one "Christmas dress and matching shoe" shopping and lunch. I took each of them to different department stores to avoid having them picking the same dress or have the saleswomen watching me trot in three different young girls into the dressing room to try on five to seven dresses each and report me for being a pedophile. It was great fun.

During our shopping spree I told each of the girls that they could pick out a dress with matching shoes or two dresses with no shoes, because my wife taught me a long time ago that the shoes cost more than the dress. Shiloh and Emmie, clearly BiBi's granddaughters, chose the shoes and proved BiBi right. I must admit that I was shocked when Sadie (red-headed twin) rejected the shoes and the second dress to buy Christmas presents for her sister and cousin. We wondered around the mall together, rode the carousel, and finally found what we were looking for at Claire's: three identical, pink, sparkly cases stuffed with makeup. When we finally got to the front of the long line, the salesgirl said that they had a "buy three get three free" sale. Not wanting to repeat the line, we picked a makeup bundle near the same price by the checkout counter, and the girls were double blessed. They each had a smaller pack to play with immediately and the pink case for Christmas. Sadie was so proud that when she walked into the house, she told her sister that she had selected a gift for her over shoes and that "it's not makeup."

As we celebrate the birth of our Savior, our goal is to be abundantly generous with our time and gifts and pass all the glory to God. I pray that this season of celebration brings you great health and joy, as we give to those around us.

December 18, 2020

A few days ago, I was listening to some music and John Mayer's song "Gravity" came on. I've heard it dozens of times, but this time I started thinking about the meaning of his words. I interpret them to say that as we live our life there is a gravitational pull, a worldly pull, to achieve and acquire more and that the more success we have the more it dilutes our previous accomplishments to secure the things that we really want and need. He sings that "Twice as much ain't twice as good and can't sustain like half could." I think he is saying that our quest for more leaves us no time to appreciate and enjoy what we have, that this quest is a vicious trap: "Gravity has taken better men than me." Is he warning us not to fall into the trap, the false values the world pulls us into?

Gravity holds our feet to the ground; it is a good thing unless you are a basketball or volleyball player. It is the strongest pull on us, and it takes the thrust of rocket engines, along with intentionality, creativity, planning, and design, to break it. It is the most powerful force we face. Or is it? Does not the gravity of the sun hold the whole earth and its inhabitants in place, in the perfect orbit to sustain life as we know it? The gravity of the sun works quietly in the background mostly unnoticed.

It struck me that the analogy between Mayer's worldly gravitational pull and actual gravity have even more in common. Just as the sun has superior gravitational pull as compared to the earth, so the Son's pull is superior to the world's. Mayer sings about how gravity (the world) pulls him down and how it has "taken better men than" him and then, perhaps subconsciously, he makes a petition, a plea, to "keep me where the light is." He repeats this multiple times at the end of his song. Or is it a confession?

We can't help but feel the gravitational pull of the world, but do you also feel the gravitational pull of the Son? Are you being swept away in the gravitational current of the world and uncertain what you can do about it? If so it's time to follow John Mayer's solution: look for and stay in the light of our Savior, Jesus Christ. This is a strategy that works for an estimated 2.4 billion people living in the world today. This strategy comes with a promise. "Seek, and you will find; knock, and it will be opened to you. For everyone who asks receives, and he who seeks finds, and to him who knocks it will be opened. (Matthew 7:7-8 NKJV)

Lord as we celebrate this season of remembering the birth of Your Son, Jesus, "the light of the world" (John 8:12), we pray for strength and wisdom in resisting the pull of the world and wisdom as we seek Your light.

January 14, 2021

Due to my recent sabbatical from Facebook, I've had several people reach out to see how we are doing. First, let me apologize if I have caused any worry. I have mostly been lazy mixed with some busy work and generally avoiding all the negativity dominating Facebook.

I just got results back from my recent scan and while the growth of my cancer continues to be slow, it is also progressing steadily. The eight measurable growths in my lungs each grew between 1 and 2 millimeters. The twenty or so spots in my lungs remain unmeasurable. I am about to start my third straight year of chemo here at the end of January. Our faith remains strong, and our eyes are fixed on the prize while we continue to be overwhelmed by your prayers and support.

Barbara is doing fantastic and is as beautiful as ever. Even though there is now no evidence of the cancer in her pancreas or liver, she is continuing to get chemo every other week like me. This was a chemo week for both of us, and we are doing pretty well with little side effects.

Due to the information we have recently collected, we have revised some of our travel plans for the first half of the year. We canceled our traditional two-week vacation in Cabo in February but are putting together a few shorter trips here in the US to connect and catch up with some friends and attend some family events.

My prayer is that 2021 has already started well for you all and that it will be a year of great personal and spiritual growth. I have never been more certain that our Lord is always with us, and I take comfort in knowing that.

God Bless you all.

February 1, 2021

For the past eight to ten years Barbara and I have been blessed to visit Cabo for a couple of weeks near the beginning of the year, while the whales are visiting. It is one of my happy places, but this year, on the advice of our oncologist, we canceled our trip due to increased risk of infection due to our low white blood cell counts. I started to wonder if I would ever visit Cabo again. *Wonder* the verb is defined as being curious about something. While many that knew me during my college years might question this next statement, but I believe my curiosity and wonder have been a driving force for me throughout my life. Even before I knew the Lord, my life was an adventure. I loved going to new places, facing new challenges, exploring uncertainty, sometimes winning and sometimes failing (learning)—wondering with every new step how it would all turn out.

In 1991, at the age of thirty-eight—I met my Savior, Jesus, and I started on a new, transformational path, slowly moving away from my plans and trying to understand and adopt His plans for me. This part of my journey was filled with even more wonder as I found myself in places, doing things that I had never imagined (like writing these posts). From the beginning I wondered if I was worthy, good enough, and prepared enough. I became aware of my greed, judgment of others, lack of forgiveness, my sin and hypocrisy. I wondered when my Lord would give up on me and kick me to the curb. Over time I learned that our God changes wonder from a verb to a noun. *Wonder*, the noun, means a cause of astonishment or admiration, the quality of exciting, amazed admiration at something awesomely mysterious or new to one's experience. God changes the wonder of our uncertainty into something wonderful. Throughout the Bible the word *wonder* is used to describe miracles by Jesus, his disciples, and the prophets. We wonder how things are going to turn out while He already knows how He is going to turn our uncertainty into blessings for us and Glory for Him.

In this season of my life, I find my curiosity for many of the things I used to wonder about waning. Many things seem less important and other wonders have been answered. It has been an interesting time for me as I have realized over the past couple of months that as my wondering has diminished my wandering (sometimes aimlessly) has increased. I feel I have experienced some spiritual stagnation and am taking steps to address my attitude. I am starting a new daily devotional with my wife, redoubling my prayer life, seeking to spend more time with my Christian brothers and sisters, and am looking for local (neighborly) situations where I might be able to help others.

Perhaps some of you may feel a little stagnated in your spiritual walk with the Lord. If so, I urge you to google "overcoming spiritual stagnation" and following some of the suggestions as we seek together to find that sweet spot in our relationship with Christ. God bless you all!

February 5, 2021

When our daughter, Allie, started dating back in high school, she brought home a few frogs (or reptile types) in her effort to find her prince. As a parent it was difficult to accept that your child could find something in these young boys worth her time, but you quickly learn not to say anything negative as that would just strengthen her desire to prove the new relationship was worthy. Frequently she would then declare that we "don't know anything." We had much better success when we encouraged them to spend more time together and then let Allie ultimately come to the same conclusion as she learned more about the young man's flaws.

They say absence makes the heart grow fonder, but what should we expect when we spend virtually all our time together? How does constant togetherness make the heart grow? I looked up antonyms for *fonder* and got results like *unloving, indifferent, uncaring, unresponsive, passionless,* and *distant.*

This pandemic has pushed us together with the people we love most, and if you are like me, it has created and/or exposed some small conflicts, or as Barbara would say, "opportunities" to improve our relationship. This is not to say our marriage is in any kind of trouble. We have been married more than forty-two years, and I wouldn't trade it for the world, but all this time spent together has shined a light on some expectations that I apparently have been missing. I am guessing over the past year I am not alone in this discovery. Can I get an amen?

I fully understand that women are complicated. I have spent perhaps fifty-five out of my sixty-seven years working to educate myself. I have accepted the changes I needed to make, honed the art of asking for forgiveness, built pedestals, learned to make celebrations of birthdays and holidays grandiose, and accepted the encroachment on my third of the closet. Honestly, I was a little surprised that I apparently still have quite a bit more to learn. I am doing a Dennis and Barbara Rainey devotional with Barbara, and they describe the difference between romancing women and men. For women you need to wine her, dine her, call her, cuddle with her, surprise her, compliment her, shop with her, listen to her talk, buy flowers, hold her hand, write love letters, and be willing to go to the ends of the earth and back again for her. To romance men, you just need to arrive naked and bring food.

Men, we have our work cut out for us, and the virus has not been our friend. The good news is that Valentine's Day is coming, and we have an opportunity to make up for this past year. Take my advice and study the list above on romancing women. Find some things that you are comfortable with and make sure you deliver on one or two of them. Please don't go overboard and make the rest of us look bad.

Of course, I am kidding. These women that the Lord gave us deserve to be loved and romanced fully, and I am going to work on delivering all twelve of the suggestions on the list, though I am struggling with ideas to communicate that I would go to the ends of the earth and back for her. The only example that I can even think of is Jesus, who came to earth and went to the cross and back, the greatest act of love ever.

I pray that your Valentine's Day is filled with love.

February 10, 2021

Who do you listen too? Who is your most trusted consultant when you have a big, or even a little, decision to make? Is your source trustworthy, or did you choose them because they don't challenge the decisions you really want to make? Do you make bad decisions? Have you ever been in a difficult place and asked yourself, "How did I get here?" Do you have friends that come to you and challenge you about the decisions you are making? Have you ever gone to a friend and challenged them about poor decisions they are making? Why is it easier to see a disastrous situation taking place or about to happen with our friends when we can't see it when it is about to happen to us?

Proverbs says "The prudent see danger and seek refuge, but the simple keep going and pay the penalty" (Proverbs 27:12). I have been in the simple column more times than I would like to admit, and I have already confessed to hundreds (maybe thousands) of times over the years. How many times during my college years at Duke did I listen to my friend and stay up for one or more beers when I had an early morning class? My trusted adviser followed me to Dallas, encouraging me to marry my college girlfriend because I needed something stable as I started my train-wreck of a career that just about everybody but me saw coming. Over the years I have foolishly invested in get-rich-quick schemes (new method of mining gold or diamond smuggling out of Sierra Leone), overextended myself in can't-miss real estate ventures, or made choices that caused difficult pain and stress on my marriage, all with full support and guidance of my counselor. I have discovered that my counselor, the one I have trusted my whole life, is a liar. In fact, he is the biggest liar I have ever experienced. Perhaps you have a liar guiding you in important decisions.

By now many of you have figured out that the liar in my life is *me*, the passions of my heart. Jeremiah wrote that "the heart is deceitful above all things and beyond cure. Who can understand it?" (Jeremiah 17:9). The truth is, my bad decisions are on me. I want more than I need while overlooking the variables that are destined to lead to some future failure or disappointment. I have learned that I can convince myself of virtually anything, and my decisions often prevent me from getting where I want to go and being who I want to be—and who God wants me to be.

How can we prevent our deceitful hearts from deceiving us? I have learned that to prevent myself from later asking, "what was I thinking?" I need to stop and think before making my decision. I use two questions to help me decide: (1) Why is this the best choice for me? And (2) Am I really being honest with myself? Question 2 is important to identify if I am thinking with my head or am I following my heart. Most of the time I know the right answer, but sometimes I struggle to follow it. I have also learned to listen to my trusted friends when they firmly question me about my decisions, reapplying the two questions above. I am still a work in progress.

Lord, we ask for wisdom in the choices we make. Protect us from our deceitful hearts and give us the strength to choose what is right. We praise You for all the blessings You share with us.

February 11, 2021

Holding to my Savior as a trusted life jacket, I am going to jump in the deep water today in order to change a few hearts related to the vicious conflict going on in our country. This post is intended to challenge and target the hearts, minds, and actions of my brothers and sisters in Christ, but I hope it rings true for those reading that are not yet believers.

We are a country that is more divided than we have been at any time since the Civil War, when more that 620,000 Americans, more than in World War I, World War II, Korea, and Vietnam combined, gave their lives. We are divided by gender, economics, education, worldview, environmental convictions, voting beliefs, immigration, religion, and, perhaps the most challenging, race, where people—I'll call them extremist—with opposite points of view continue to drive conflict and take lives. I believe race is the most difficult challenge we still face, so I am going to try challenging you (Christians) to embrace our biblical teachings to help transform our country (the world) to be more like heaven.

The great Dr. Martin Luther King Jr. said, "Injustice anywhere is a threat to justice everywhere" and followed it up with "whatever effects one directly effects all indirectly." I believe that universal justice is impossible without universal truth. Here is where I know I am going to step on a few toes because I have many passionate friends with strong beliefs surrounding all these issues, but the *truth* is never found in the often-messy middle. We collect our facts to support and wall off our point of view, but facts don't replace fear or change hearts, only experience does that. Being non-racist is not enough for the church. We must be anti-racist in the same way we are anti-abuse, anti-abortion, or anti-bullying.

This begs two questions (stolen from Andy Stanley): (1) How *do* people that don't look like me (believe what I believe) experience me? And (2) How *should* they experience me? Jesus said, "A new commandment I give you: love one another. As I have loved you, you must love one another" (John 13:34), and the apostle Paul wrote, "Carry each other's burdens, and in this way you will fulfill the law of Christ" (Galatians 6:2). Whose burdens are you carrying? Do they look exclusively like you (question for Christ followers of all races).

These principles call and challenge all Christ followers to reach out lovingly to their neighbor regardless of the earthly (meaningless in heaven) conflicts and help them carry their burdens, so they can fulfill the law of your Savior.

Lord, today we ask for a spirit of putting aside the things that separate us from our neighbors and adopting an attitude of love and forgiveness toward them that will glorify You Lord. Help us to see our neighbors' burdens and give us the courage to reach out in love to help carry them. All the glory goes to You!

February 18, 2021

They say that hindsight is twenty-twenty, but if that were the case there would never be any disagreements about instant replay decisions, the success and desirability of communism or socialism, or who wore it better. The truth is that we all carry subtle (or not so subtle) personal biases about everything based upon our past experiences, no matter how objective we claim to be. These factors along with our quests for more power, followers, and love provide the primary source for most of the conflict we participate in today. We falsely think that we can change minds and hearts if we can just get the other guy or gal to just stop and listen for fifteen minutes or maybe just read our Facebook posts. I am a perfect example of this misguided behavior because my hindsight has confirmed to me that only God changes people's hearts and minds.

Barbara and I recently started a daily couples devotional which has opened a deep dialog between us. The other day as we were talking about our relationship and how our Lord has so faithfully brought us through it together, I shared with her for the first time that if God had waited any longer (the end of 1991) to reach me, our marriage would not have survived and our lives today would be so much different—less joyful, less connected, less impactful. Let me explain.

I married Barbara in December of '78, and like all newlyweds we were excited about starting our life together and building a family. Life was fun until it got harder, until children came. We both began to sacrifice parts of ourselves as we raised our children and built our home, family, and business. Then something terrible happened: we had some success, and our original dreams and goals were no longer sufficient. More success meant more travel, and I was spending one hundred or more nights a year on the road for business. Out of those one hundred nights I was entertaining (cocktails, dinner, cocktails) around 75 percent of the time. On top of that I probably added another fifteen to twenty nights a year at off-site partner retreats and self-planned client development events, boondoggles in places like Maui and Malibu. Somewhere early along the way my sacrifice (really Barbara's sacrifice) to grow our business turned into a lifestyle that I embraced. Add in the decadent industry we were focused on, selling high-fi equipment and emerging video game and computer products to retailers, it was life in the fast lane. And while I worked hard to be a good father when I was home Barbara got the leftover energy and attention.

I wanted to be a good husband, but I was not. We went through counseling, and I knew what I needed to do but my stubborn deceitful heart (sounds like BS to me too) overwhelmed my desire to do what was right. I felt helpless and ultimately doomed. Have you ever felt like this? Where you knew your current direction was taking you down the path of destruction but couldn't find a way to save yourself from yourself? That's where I was, and as I looked for solutions I was not looking or even considering that Jesus was the answer. By the end of 1991 my heart and my head were captured by my Savior. Barbara and I got on the same page regarding our belief and faith in Jesus, and before long I had confessed everything to her and began a long path to rebuild her trust. Now we are able to talk about how we were back then. The Boomer and Barbara from before 1991 are unrecognizable.

The moral is that if you are struggling with your relationships—marriage, business, or children—and what you have been doing isn't working, seek the Lord. He is the only One who can change our deceitful hearts. He changed my hardened heart, and He can change yours.

Lord, we pray as we confront the struggles and challenges of life that we will have the wisdom to turn to You and Your word and overcome the barriers that separate us from You and each other.

March 9, 2021

Last weekend I attended my five-year-old granddaughter Emmie's first soccer game of the season. Her team, Rainbow Dash, played at a complex with over twenty fields all being used. It was alive with parents, families, and players as games were played while the previous teams organized to leave and players for the next game were arriving to warm up. It was awesome, and except for a few people wearing masks, it was one of my first experiences that I would call normal over the past year. It was very encouraging.

I remembered my granddaughters first season in the fall of 2019 when they were all three years old. Their team's name was Hot Dogs, but I thought they should have been called the Blind Squirrels because somehow they managed to score a few goals. Emmie and Sadie walked around the field holding hands and talking only moving quickly to get out of the way of the ball and the beehive following it. Shiloh our other granddaughter just kind of followed the ball around making no attempt to advance it or defend. Being the easygoing, uncompetitive guy that I am I was inclined to just sit back, enjoy my coffee, offer calm words of encouragement, and let her collect her trophy at the end of the season. I don't know what came over me, but that is not what I did. After challenging their coaches (my son and "son in love") to no avail, by halftime of the second game I had seen enough and pulled the girls together and told them that I would give them one dollar for every time they kicked the ball in the second half. Sadie and Emmie smiled, held hands, and went out to stroll around for the field for second half. Shiloh, however, with her eyes on a new pair of Elsa shoes, ran out and within the first minute or so made contact with the ball at the far end of the field. She turned and made a beeline down the field to where I was sitting to collect her dollar, making enough noise so that everyone at the field could figure out what was happening. It was a little embarrassing for me, but that day she fleeced me for eight dollars and progressed through the season.

I remember how proud she was running toward me to collect her reward for something that she should have done without any incentive, but the quid pro quo motivated her to act. This idea of you do this for me and I'll do this for you is part of the everyday human experience. We all accept and do this in one form or another with our friends, family, coworkers, bosses, politicians, contractors, and most religions. It is an accepted universal practice here in America and throughout the world.

The one exception I can think of is Christianity. Jesus went to the cross to cover our sin for generations of people who were never even born. He suffered for our iniquities (sin for UNC grads) without asking anything of us. He showed us the way we can conquer death. "It is by grace we have been saved, through faith—and this is not from ourselves, it is the gift of God—not by works, so that no one can boast" (Ephesians 2:8-9). All we must do is believe that Jesus is the Christ, the Son of the living God, and put our faith and trust in him. He has already done all the work and regardless of any of your past, current, and future circumstances, His gift is available to all who believe in Him.

March 18, 2021

Many of you have heard me talk about interviewing the boys that wanted to date my daughter, Allie. Until the middle of her senior year of high school, any boy that wanted to date her had to call me and set up a meeting. During our discussion I highlighted that the purpose of our discussion was for them to get to know me so that they would understand the parameters of going out with her and the risks of drifting outside the lines. They needed to know that they would be taking over the responsibility for her welfare, which ultimately was mine, and that they would be held personally accountable for both their actions and/or Allie's when she was with them. We discussed everything from hand placement, disrobing, truth telling, smoking, drinking, drug use and anything sexual in nature. These conversations gave me the opportunity to share that if they violated any of these principles that I would find them and hold them accountable. We discussed in a general way what that meant, and I am certain that none of them were confused.

Parents instinctively know that it is our responsibility to love, protect, train, educate, disciple, and encourage our children as we prepare them to be successful. We prepare their room before they are born and most of us would take a bullet for them. We also know that they will stumble and fail; they will need our forgiveness, love, and emotional support. From experience we also understand that each of our children must make a choice and that some will choose drugs, alcohol, violence, and/or theft. Despite their children's poor choices, parents continue to love their children, but after giving them chance after chance ultimately realize they need to pull back and let them suffer (hit bottom). They need to hope and wait for their children to reject the attitudes and decisions that led to their failure and turn back to the values that their parents discipled them with.

Of course, these principles break down in the real world because the luckiest of all children have imperfect parents and many are raised without mothers while even more are raised without fathers. We know that the bigger the breakdown of the family unit, the bigger the chance for breakdowns in the children.

This human parental failure clarifies why we need a heaven both here on earth and for the opportunity to spend eternity with our Creator. Like our earthly parents our heavenly Father loves, educates, trains, encourages, and disciples us. Before we were born, He created our homes both here and in heaven, and instead of taking a bullet for us, He took nails and died on a cross to pay the penalty for our sins if we turn back to Him and repent from making our own personal desires more important than his. But unlike our earthly fathers, He is a perfect Father with a perfect plan for us, but it is up to us to choose. Have you chosen well? Are you happy and confident about your eternal future? If not, He is still waiting patiently for you to repent and choose Him. What is holding you back?

May 17, 2021

Back in January I wrote a post about my daughter, Allie, treating me like I was already gone. I told her to calm down and enjoy these times because every day is a gift from God. To make my point with her I said, "I am not circling the drain yet." Instead of "circling the drain" she heard "circling the dream," and I wrote about how much better and more accurate "dream" was. After all the Bible describes heaven as a place that has unimaginable beauty. When you think about all the beautiful places God has created around the world and universe, what is left that hasn't been imagined? Of course, this is human nature. Even when God says you can't imagine it, the first thing we do is start imagining. This imagination becomes part of our awake dream of what heaven will be, thus, circle the dream.

Recently I was reading an article and it used the phrase "circling the promise." I spent some time dwelling on it and concluded that the word *promise* was way more accurate than *dream*. A wonderful promise is much more desirable than a dream. It was at this point I realized that Christians have already received the promise when we gave our lives to Christ; we are no longer circling it.

I also rethought what it meant to circle the dream and to whom and how it might apply. The answer became obvious to me that the people who are really circling the dream are those who are not yet Christians. Everyone is programmed to dream about finding the path that creates the best version of ourselves, but the question is: Are our dreams trustworthy? I think we all know the answer to that question (no for you Carolina fans). Therefore, Jesus gave us the tools to shine a light on the promise so it will be visible to the dreamers. He said that we should love our neighbors like we love God and that we should share our stories, our testimony of what God has done for us.

HEALTH UPDATE: I have been on a little sabbatical for the past few months as we both have had some nagging health issues. (I was in the hospital on three separate occasions over a five-week period.) During this time, we circled our wagons a little, but we have realized that we really need to get back to our old habits. It is tough to help others when you are focused inwardly, so our plan is to start engaging with more people. Thank you for your prayers and support.

Lord, thank You for the ways that You love us all the way to Your final promise to us, the kingdom of heaven. Please help us to love the people that have not yet discovered Your plans for them all the way to Jesus so that they might trade a dream for a promise.

May 23, 2021

How are you doing? This is easily the most asked question I hear from my friends and family, especially since our children are all on their own and have stopped asking for money. Perhaps it is just my own personal assumption but when I hear that question, I feel like I am being asked for a medical update. I welcome the question because it always gives me a chance to share what God has been doing during this difficult season of life and all the ways we are being blessed as we deal with the medical issues surrounding our treatment. It is a fair question, and I know it is always asked out of concern and compassion for us.

This morning Pastor Joe preached on this question from a different point of view from my post here, but it made me stop and reflect on how I am doing. Joe's message was targeted at people who are perhaps struggling with emotional issues. You just look at Facebook to see how many people are angry, feel discriminated against, fearful, discouraged, lonely, divided, and depressed. Yet, if you asked most of these people, "How are you doing," they would respond with, "Great!" (Many times, Barbara responds to me with, "Fine!") For some reason we feel compelled to guard are responses. Joe's sermon was about where you go and what you can do to overcome these emotions that rob us of God's desire for us to live a life full of joy, hope, and peace.

So how am I doing? I am doing so much more than fighting a difficult battle with cancer and sharing my testimony of how our Creator is keeping us comforted during this storm—even though there is nothing more important than telling the world about what God has done for me and can do for them. The emotions I am feeling most are hope, compassion, love, gratefulness, and confidence.

I have *hope*, not for a cure, though that would be great, but hope that I still have some great days, weeks, months, and perhaps years ahead of me—time to continue to share fantastic experiences and love with my family, friends, and loved ones.

I feel *compassion* for all the people who are lost and struggling to find hope, peace, and love, the people who are struggling with the issues Pastor Joe preached on and those who are struggling with medical or physical issues like me. It is difficult to watch so many people struggle, especially my Christian brothers and sisters.

I feel massively loved. For the past five years I know that a network of loved ones has dedicated hundreds or thousands of prayers (perhaps millions) petitioning our Creator on our behalf. You have shown up with food, helped with repairs around our house, and loved on us in so many ways. Barbara and I also love you and have a heart to do whatever we can to demonstrate that love.

We are beyond grateful for the ways you have overwhelmed us with your love in action. We are also overwhelmed by the way God connected us to love and support each other as his angels and ambassadors.

I am also *confident* of the path we are going down. We know that there is likely more pain and suffering in the not-too-distant future, but we will never suffer as much as Christ willingly suffered for us. And He told us that in order to follow him, we need to carry our own cross, a symbol of suffering. I am also confident that the path we are on leads us to the gates of heaven.

So, the next time you see me, and I may not look so good, and if you ask me the question "How are you doing?" you can expect to hear a more complicated response when I answer, "Great"!

My prayer for all of you tonight is that if someone asks you, "How are you doing" you can honestly answer them, "Great!"

June 10, 2021

Back in the late eighties we were traveling as a family to a ski trip in Steamboat Springs, Colorado, which required us to change planes in Denver. Our new plane was a much smaller prop plane with about twenty rows and two seats on each side. I sat with Allie who was about six years old at the time, and Barbara was with Ivan, who was three. Shortly before takeoff the flight attendant announced that they were expecting heavy turbulence, and there would be no cabin service during the flight. As we flew over the mountains the plane was tossed around frequently falling up to a hundred feet at a time followed by a big bang when it hit the updraft current. Barbara and the kids all looked to me for a comforting comment as passengers around us screamed and reached for the bags in the seat pouch. Not knowing what to say I just looked down at Allie and said, "This is like a roller coaster; hold your hands up" as I lifted mine. We bounced again and Allie screamed with laughter shouting to Ivan, "Ivan, it's a roller coaster. Hold your hands up." Ivan was obedient and started laughing during the next free fall. Barbara sat white-knuckled, grasping the armrests with all her strength. While several other passengers joined the children in their laughter, most were frightened or ill.

Recently I have been thinking a lot about fear. Some of that has been driven by our health issues, but mostly it it's a result of just watching how our society is changing, how as a nation we are becoming more afraid. Over the past year people have been afraid to leave their home, take or keep a job as a policeman, enforce laws when faced with rioting mobs (afraid to call them anything but peaceful protests), open schools, speak their minds without getting cancelled. What has happened to us? Why are we so fearful? Have you taken time to stop and examine the things you are afraid of? Are they really that scary or are they more like our plane ride filled with unexpected bumps that ultimately had no effect on our ski trip other than insuring we arrived.

Through self-examination I have come to believe that fear is the result of my plans conflicting with God's plan for me. Despite my faith and my desire to serve our Creator I recognize that I have plans for my life for what is coming next, where I want to go and what I want to do and with whom I want to do it. This agenda has been part of my marriage, family, work, retirement, education, and faith. Yet, despite my best plans, there have been times when something happened to disrupt my vision for each of these areas causing me to *fear* and worry about how I could ever overcome the setbacks. Despite all these past disasters and interruptions, I can look back at all my wasted energy being afraid and say my life has been great, God has been great. As a Christian I know how our heavenly story ends, but I let these issues that cause me to fear to camouflage the ending and lose sight of my destiny. Our setbacks generally fall into two categories, self-inflicted or God pruning us for future conquests for His glory. The Bible tells us 365 times not to be afraid, that we are to fear not.

These are the thoughts that Barbara and I cling to as we work to celebrate our lives daily. When we ride the roller coaster of life, we want to raise our hands to embrace the gifts and opportunities that God makes available to us and give Him thanks for all of it. We cannot let fear get in the way of our love of Christ.

June 13, 2021

About two years ago BiBi and I were watching a movie with our twin granddaughters at their house. Suddenly there was a very loud crack of thunder as one of our famous Texas storms was moving through the area. Almost instantly the girls moved closer, and their lab jumped on the couch and tried to get between the girls and us. I asked if they were frightened by the thunder. They nodded. I put a big smile on my face and told them that whenever I hear thunder it makes me want to dance and stood up and began to dance around the room (so glad there were no cameras). In no time the girls had joined me and even their dog Milo got up and wandered between us trying to understand what was going on.

I thought that this was an interesting metaphor about how we respond to the storms in our life. The apostle Mark tells the story of Jesus and several of his disciples crossing a lake when a great storm arose" and began tossing the boat. Jesus was sleeping during this and the disciples woke him saying "Teacher don't you care that we are perishing?" This is how many of us respond to the storms in our life. We overreact as we jump straight to the worst possible scenario, believing that Jesus doesn't know, understand, or care about our dangerous circumstances. Jesus, don't you care? We forget just how much Jesus cares. We suddenly have amnesia about the cross and the promise of heaven. When they woke Jesus, he rebuked the wind and then said to his disciples, "Why are you so afraid?" Do you still have no faith?" (Mark 4:36-40).

How do you respond in the storms of life? Some people hide, some respond with anger, some people turn to alcohol or drugs, some try to escape by taking their own lives, some will lie, some will run, and I'm sure you can think of more. All these responses are based on fear that God is not who he says he is, or maybe we just don't have the right kind of trusting relationship with him. Again, how do you respond?

God uses storms to test and perfect our faith. He tests us, not because he wants to give us a grade or a gold star but because he wants each of us to understand how far we still must go. He doesn't want us to sleepwalk thru life falsely believing that we already have all the faith we need. Just like the disciples, I am clearly lacking faith and need more testing. He also uses storms to strengthen our testimony. Five years ago, I had no idea how to even talk with someone fighting and struggling with cancer. Now I talk with people battling cancer almost daily, encouraging them and sharing how God is pulling me through very challenging circumstances, how he is a blessing in the storm.

We have many choices in the way we respond to the storms of our lives. Will we fear or will we dance when the storm settles in above us? Will we hide or will we pray? Will we push away from our creator, or will we lean into his strength, love, and promises? Will we withdraw or will we celebrate?

My prayer is that we will choose worship over worry, celebration over disappointment, and faith over fear.

June 17, 2021

As Barbara and I continue to ride this roller coaster called life, full of ups and downs with twists and turns, we strive to take each day as a blessing, living with anticipation of what God has planned for us next. As we approach the crest of the peak, not knowing what is coming, we take our hands off the safety bar and lift them skyward, trusting and believing the promises of our Creator. Our faith in this is strong despite the difficult challenges we've faced, because our Lord has always brought us through our past crises. His track record is perfectly intact.

This past Tuesday morning, with our hands lifted high, it felt like our roller coaster had an unexpected power outage leaving us hanging upside down and reaching for our safety bars. We learned that Barbara's recent scan revealed that her fast-growing cancer had exploded well beyond her initial diagnosis, expanding in both the pancreas and liver and traveling to her lungs with multiple growths. The pills she had been taking were ineffective in everything except making her feel bad. We were not surprised by the return but were overwhelmingly surprised by the quantity and the speed at which it had expanded.

The good news is that we have a history with this specific type of cancer, and we know that prayer combined with the chemo infusions Barbara took previous were extremely successful in shrinking the previous growths. There is a high expectation that this success will be repeated as she started her infusions again this past Tuesday. Because of the rapid rate of growth, we really have just this one chance to knock it back.

When our doctor left the room, we let go of the safety bar and just stood there holding and tearfully comforting each other. Then we realized nothing really had changed. This information did not add or subtract a single day from the life God planned for us and that He would heal us either here or in heaven. We left the doctor's office.

Barbara headed to the infusion room to get her chemo cocktail, and I headed home to start sharing our information with family and friends. We were both back on the coaster, arms reaching up and thanking God for the gift of another day.

We ask for your continued prayers that the chemo will be effective, the side effects of the chemo will not be overwhelming, and for wisdom in choosing the decisions that will come.

We thank you for your continued prayers and support and pray that this post finds you with your hands held high.

June 28, 2021

In mid-August of 1971 I packed my bags and headed to Durham to begin football practice and start my college experience. One of the early surprising experiences took place the day before classes were to begin. Most of the male freshman lived in House P, which was right across the quad from the Phi Delts and ATOs. Several upperclassmen gathered the freshman on the quad and stated that there was an annual tradition. The Freshman needed to work their way over to Haines House (the nursing dorm) and execute a panty raid. I had no idea what a panty raid consisted of but being someone who supports tradition, I was curious to go along and see what it was about. Several older students lead us through campus and the Duke hospital to the place where we were going to "occupy" Haines House. Yes, long before occupying cities, buildings, and capitals became a "thing," we were the front runners.

As we got to the front of the dorm the housemother came out, stood on the front steps, held her hand out, and told everyone to stop.

About two hundred of us did just that. As she was instructing us to turn around and go home, one of my new best friends (Hugh) says to me, "There is only one of her. There is no way she can stop us." He grabbed my arm and started running toward the front door. Having no plan of my own, I just followed him, and the rest of the pack followed me. In no time we were all inside running up and down the halls with no idea what we were doing. Many of the (probably frightened) girls locked themselves in their rooms while others stood in their doorways or huddled together in the hall in a low traffic area, perhaps excited about the prospects of having their panties raided.

It was all over in about fifteen minutes. As we walked back to our dorms, the general discussion was that the whole experience was overrated. Outside of a few small race riots in my high school, this was my first experience with mob mentality. I found myself in a place that I never planned to be, following someone (Hugh) whose objectives I did not know, and was literally doing something that I was a little uncomfortable with because a bunch of guys that I had just met said we should do it.

Today, mobs usually have leaders that plan an "occupation" and rioting, but most of the people following them were like me, just going with the flow and find themselves led into circumstances that entrap them.

There is a lesson here. First, before standing with any group that promotes violence or anarchy like the Proud Boys, BLM, Antifa, KKK, learn about their leaders and what they stand for. Know what their written goals, methods, and objectives are. Second, think about what your values and goals are and match them against the group's. If you march with them and the result is chaos, destruction, and death, then you are unnecessarily putting yourself at risk and giving yourself a label that you may have to carry the rest of your life. Finally, look at the history of groups that you think you want to join, what were the results that were left in their wake. Would you be proud to stand up and take credit for them or would you be embarrassed to tell you children or your grandmother.

Like me, I am guessing that many of you believe our country has many opportunities to improve in so many areas, but I think most you would also have to agree that the actions of our government and citizens over the past decade or more has been counterproductive in addressing the important issues that confront us.

Lord, I pray that You would give us all wisdom to discriminate between right and wrong, good and bad, mercy and condemnation, peace and conflict, and love and hatred. Please help us to choose our leaders and our friends wisely and send Your Spirit to guide us toward the path that You want us to take.

July 8, 2021

A couple of weeks ago we had our immediate family together for a casual take-out dinner. BiBi was talking with our five-year-old granddaughters when Emmie crawled onto BiBi's lap and asked her what her favorite thing in the whole world was, instructing her that she could only pick one. She said, "That is easy. God is my favorite thing in the world." Then BiBi asked Sadie, our red-headed granddaughter the same question. She thought for a second and then said. "My favorite thing is God, with a snow cone." I had to laugh and at the same time admire her answer. I loved that she has connected God as the giver of gifts. She could have easily asked me, after all I am an instrument that God uses to bless Sadie and our other grandchildren. I also love that she asked for such a small gift, content in this moment of her life. There is no request that is too small or too big for our Lord. In fact, our most severe challenges are like snow cones for the Creator of the heavens.

I thought about what a perfect picture this is of my relationship with my heavenly Father. At times, when pleading for my Provider to help me out, I've even caught myself reminding God of my effort to be His faithful servant. Fortunately for me God does not remind me of all the times I have stumbled and failed to be faithful. His list would surely be many multiples of times larger than my list of my faithful deeds. I am also certain that my list of unanswered prayers pales in comparison to His list of answered prayers, many of them answered before I ever spoke a word or formed a thought, the prayers I would be making if my Lord had not already blessed me. I also believe that my unanswered and delayed prayers have and are preparing me to receive our ultimate reward, eternity with our Father in heaven.

One of our friends sent us a book on heaven which shared a perspective that I had never considered before. It made the point that for faithful Christians, our time here on earth is as close to hell as we will ever be, and by contrast, for nonbelievers, their time on earth is as close to heaven as they will ever be.

Lord, we bring our prayers to You, asking for the things we believe will make our lives better and more secure when You already know what we really need is *You* and that Your eternal plan for us is better than anything else we could imagine. For everyone that reads this post, I pray that their time here on earth is as close as they ever get to hell.

Just an FYI, Sadie's prayer has been answered as we have ordered a snow cone machine for our Allie's birthday.

July 19, 2021

Last week our son Ivan and his wife, Leah, asked if BiBi and I could relieve Leah's parents on Wednesday afternoon to watch Emmy and Mike III. It was BiBi's chemo week, and she was not up to it, so I went alone. Our children married great spouses from great families, and her parents decided to stay, perhaps they were questioning my readiness. It was a great afternoon because I got to spend quality time talking with Mimo and Ditto and got focused time with my grandchildren.

We found a new game as I played with twenty-one-month-old Mike. He had recently discovered the meaning of "belly button" and was determined to pull up my oversized T-shirt (lost sixty pounds) and put his finger in mine. As he moved in, I grabbed the front of my shirt, pulling it over his head and shoulders and then gave him a big squeeze. As I lifted my shirt, he had a big grin on his face and said, "More." In no time his grin turned into a giggle and then to full out laughter as he continued to call out for more. The only thing sweeter than a child's laughter is when that child is yours or one of your children's. It was a day worth living for, like so many others.

"More" was the first word that Ivan learned, and it is one of the first words our children learn. Without "more" it would be difficult to teach them "please." I don't remember when I learned "more," but I expect it was one of my first words, and "more" has been a central theme at every different stage of my life. Sometimes it was more food or toys. Other times is was more money, success, power, love, friends, house, car, or championships. Most recently, I cry out for more time and energy and more healing and more weight. I'm encouraged by God's promise and the great days God continues to provide for us, the days worth living for.

Soon our focus will shift again as we begin to seek more heaven and leave behind the pains and struggles of this world. But until then

I've learned that there is still more work to be done here, and as the number of days remaining grows shorter, we need to work even harder to share more of God's love.

July 29, 2021

Back in the early 2000s Barbara came to me and said let's go to Israel with a tour group from the local Christian radio morning personality. My initial response was, "No, I don't want to spend what little vacation time we get on going to the Holy Land. Why don't you ask Donna?" Apparently, I was predictable. She told me that she had already talked to Donna, and she was committed to going. To this day I am uncertain if I was plan A or B. About two weeks later the movie *The Bucket List* came out. I realized Israel was on my bucket list, so I changed my mind about going. It was one of the best reconsiderations I ever made. From that experience I learned that my initial instinct to new ideas usually defaulted to no.

Why do we teach our children the word "no"? Like "more" it is one of the first words babies learn and is the top catalyst word for teaching them "thank you," a phrase that needs to be used more. We could all give more gratitude. Once they learn to say no, suddenly they start rejecting food that they appeared to love just two days ago and respond to nap time with a resounding, "No!" They don't want to sit down or hold your hand walking through a parking lot. "No! No!" Once the no's start they never stop. "No, I don't want to go there." "No, I don't want to wear that." "No, I don't want to finish my dinner, get up, go to bed, do my homework, watch that, go to that college," and on and on.

But it doesn't stop there, it follows us right into adulthood. In fact, during my marriage to Barbara I'm pretty sure one of us has said no to just about everything listed from the children's list above. Except when you're older, you have more important decisions to make, you have more opportunities to say no.

Many (maybe most) of the things and ideas we say no to we eventually come back and say yes once we have matured or obtained more information. In fact, in this culture saying no is no more binding than saying yes. Like my visit to Israel, which was life changing for me, there are often blessings attached when no's turn to yeses. In Jesus tells a parable about two sons whose father asked them to work in the vineyard. One son says yes but does not do the work. The other son initially rejected his father's request (no) but after reconsidering, he showed up to do what was requested. Then Jesus asks, "Which of the two did what his father wanted?" (Mathew 21:28-31). Then He puts the parable in context telling the chief priests and the elders that the tax collectors and prostitutes will enter the kingdom of God ahead of them because they would not accept Him or do what he taught while the prostitutes and tax collectors did.

In the world (at least the US) today, more and more people are saying no to the kingdom of God (heaven), accepting instead a worldview that says we can do whatever we want without consequence. Perhaps it is time to take your first or one more deep dive into God's teaching. Barbara and I know that in the best-case scenario our time is short, but your time is getting shorter every day too. Perhaps some of you will even precede us in leaving this earth. It is time to prepare.

Lord, today I pray for all my brothers and sisters who so far have failed to put their trust in You and accept Your Word, promises, and gifts. Father, help them change their hearts and pursue a relationship with You.

❧ ❧ ❧

July 30, 2021 (1 of 2)

Last week Barbara had a new scan to measure the growth of her cancer. The results were disappointing. In fact, it was almost a worst-case scenario. All her existing growths virtually doubled in size and the quantities of growths also doubled. She now has one hundred growths just in her lungs, and it is fast growing. This week she started a new chemo regimen. The doctors hope this will give her up to another six months with some quality of life. We are looking for the right balance between chemo and cancer growth; sometimes the cure seems worse than the disease.

We are asking for continued prayer that God will give us wisdom and continue to comfort us and our family as we walk through this journey. I know that many of you are very close to Barbara, and we continue to pray for your comfort and peace as you watch your friend suffer. We remain strong in our faith and continue to lean into the promise of our Creator.

July 30, 2021 (2 of 2)

This is the third (maybe final) post on powerful and misleading words that come out of the mouths of babes and that we continue to use throughout our lives. The word today is "mine." I watch our twin granddaughters, who are surprisingly great at sharing with each other, stake out specific items they are less willing, perhaps unwilling, to share, saying, "mine."

When Allie was about five, we were playing at the pool. She loved when I would throw her in the air and she would flip around. She asked for more. Of course, several of her friends would always swim over and ask for a turn, and Allie would try and fight them off saying, "my Daddy." We claim ownership over virtually anything and everything. My house, my car, my girlfriend, my husband, my money, my idea, my job, my cancer. We claim these things as mine, but are they really ours? As an adult I have claimed ten different houses as mine. I can't count the number of cars that are no longer mine, and I'm not going to put a number on all my past girlfriends before meeting the love of my life who informed me that I was no longer, perhaps never, theirs.

We have all heard the expression "You can't take it with you." Usually we hear it from good friends who are encouraging us to be more generous. As Barbara and I approach the gates of heaven, we have done the research, and you can't rent a U-Haul to take your possessions with you. All our stuff, the things we still claim as mine have suddenly become inconvenient as we rework our will and plan to divide our assets and all the junk we have clutched firmly for all of these years. Fool's gold.

As I approach the end of the race, I wish I had learned at an earlier age the ONE THING that is mine, that will last well beyond my last breath, is my legacy. Some people look at legacies as leaving a building, an accomplishment, or a record. I don't want to minimize anybody's contributions, but for me, my legacy is my family. As a father, the things I have taught my children that will be passed down to their children and the relationships I have built is something that I own and will continue to own for generations. My legacy is far from perfect. There are so many things I could have done better as a father, but I am proud of my children and the parents they have (and will) become, the faith they have demonstrated, and the values that they hold.

Understanding this helps me understand that I am/we are the legacy of God, who claims *all* things as His, including me/us. He and He alone, as Creator, can call all things "Mine." I have experienced many great blessings in my life, but nothing compares to the realization of the presence of my heavenly Father, who claims me as His.

August 13, 2021

These past few months have been challenging for me but especially challenging for Barbara. I am writing this from her hospital room (day five) as she sleeps. She has had maybe ten hours of quality time over the past month, and the trend has not yet started to improve. She was unable to take her chemo this week, and while her cancer is an aggressive grower, she feels no better despite having ten days to flush her last chemo out of her system. We have been crying out for mercy, and like the Casting Crowns song says, "Once again I say amen, and it's still raining."

"Jesus, son of David, have mercy on me" (Mark 10:47). This was the cry of the blind man Bartimaeus as he heard Jesus approaching. Jesus prayed to the Lord asking Him to take this cup (crucifixion) from Him before giving into the Father's will. The fact is that at some point (or many points) in our lives we all need mercy. The question is where do we go to receive mercy. Can the doctors write a prescription for mercy? Can your spouse or best friend put it in a gift bag? Your parents can't bequeath it to you in their will, and it's not on the shelf at Walmart. Mercy is allusive and difficult to find if you don't know where to look.

Biblical mercy is defined as "love that responds to human need in an unexpected or unmerited way." Our sin against our Creator is what makes us "unmerited," and the unexpected response to our sin is forgiveness and the promise of eternal life with our Savior. Jesus confirms this in Mathew 10: "I desire Mercy not sacrifice. For I have not come to call the righteous, but sinners" (v. 13). This is good news for me because I don't know any righteous people, only sinners.

It is comforting that Jesus desires mercy for me, but it is also challenging for me to balance my ideas of what mercy looks like compared to God's perfect plan. Sometimes, as with the healing of blind Bartimaeus, it's clear to see God's mercy. But then there are times when God says no to our specific request for mercy as He did with His Son Jesus when He allowed Him to be arrested, tortured, and crucified. Jesus wasn't even "unmerited," so where was the mercy in that? Of course, we know that God's mercy was in Christ's suffering, to show His love for us and offset our sin and enable us to be with Him in heaven.

Mercy comes in many forms, and knowing that ultimately our final destination is heaven, our specific cry for mercy is just to end Barbara's suffering one way or the other. The Casting Crowns song goes on to reflect what I believe: "As your mercy falls, I praise the God who gives and takes away" ("I Will Praise You in the Storm," *Lifesong*, Reunion Records, 2005).

August 18, 2021

I am sure most everyone knows, but heaven gained a very amazing person yesterday.

August 20, 2021

A week ago, I posted some of my thoughts about God's mercy, a mercy that is sometimes difficult for us to see or understand from our own small, self-centered perspectives. I wrote about the choices that seemed so large standing in front of us, decisions about treatment for Barbara. We prayed for a clear direction, comfort, and peace but mostly we prayed for mercy, that her suffering would end.

Last Monday, after she spent six days in the hospital the week before, we met with our beloved oncologist and had what she called a serious conversation about the next step for Barbara. She gave us three options. In the retail world we would have called them a good, better, or best selection but none of them seemed attractive at all. We planned to come back on Tuesday with a decision, and Barbara and I went home to pray and choose. Barbara had been struggling for several months, and she was tired of suffering. For her the best solution was to end all treatments and move to hospice care. At about 8:30 we sat on our couch and prayed together that the Lord would come soon and take her. That He would end her suffering quickly. We released her body and her spirit to our Creator. She died that night peacefully in her sleep.

God's mercy and timing could not have been more perfect. He waited to take her until we both had found peace in her decision; He didn't take her until we were ready. And then He answered our pray completely and immediately, taking her in her sleep, ending her suffering forever.

Over the past few days, I have shed more than a few tears, and I expect more as the finality of her passing sinks in, but mostly I am rejoicing with and for her. It is difficult to watch the love of your life suffer physically and emotionally, and I am so grateful for God's mercy. I already miss her, but I know that I am not far behind, and we will be reunited soon, that she is with our Savior preparing a place for me.

Also, I would like to thank everyone for your kind words, thoughtful gifts of food and flowers, prayers, and encouragement. You have lifted me and our family's spirits more than you could possibly know. You are a blessing!

September 5, 2021

I would like to thank everyone for your amazing birthday wishes and prayers. I remember some difficult birthdays with two- and three-a-day football practices and learning of Barbara's cancer last year, but this first one spent without my partner in life and love has been the most difficult. Though I was certain this day was coming as I watched her deal with her cancer and chemo, there was no way to prepare for the slow destruction of a loved one's body.

It has been nineteen days since our Lord mercifully called her home in a quick and quiet end to her suffering. God answered her prayers. Since then, I have been surrounded by family and friends, but that ends tomorrow when I return home in search of a new "normal" routine. For the past forty-plus years Barbara has respectfully kept me on track as we pushed through the opportunities and challenges of life and raising a family together. She helped get me back on track whenever my immaturity and desire to push the limits of life got me off the rails. She kept me centered in God's Word and plans for us

Who is going to manage my to-do list? What will replace the nights when we just held each other and praised God for our children and grandchildren or prayed for the needs of our friends and loved ones? I struggle to take my medicine at the right time, eat enough protein, drink enough fluids, and check the mail. No one else knows the extent of the hardships and struggles that we worked through in our marriage, that made it and us stronger and pulled us even closer together.

Now I must face the future and uncertainty of my cancer without my favorite life partner and caregiver as God's plan for me takes a new and different direction. I must admit that it is a little frightening, this uncertainty about what is next. But this is not the first time (hopefully not the last) that I've just had to trust God and seek his will for me, and I am confident and encouraged that once again He will direct my steps and pull me through. That His plan for me will have purpose, hope, and love.

Regardless of anything I am feeling, I know I am not alone. God's Word and Holy Spirit comfort me and bring me peace. My family and I have grieved together but also comfort each other, and I am surrounded by a "great multitude" of friends who have shared their love and support.

Jeremiah 29:11 says, " 'For I know the plans I have for you', declares the Lord, 'plans to give you hope and a future.' ".

Again, thank you for all your love, prayers, and birthday wishes! I pray you will all join me in anticipation of what the Lord has planned for us next.

November 15, 2021

I can't believe that it has already been three months since Barbara claimed her inheritance in heaven. Individually, these ninety days have just slowly crept by, exposing all the ways I have missed her—many of which I was unprepared for. I had underestimated her impact on the quality of my everyday experience in life. Looking back, I see that I took too much of her love for granted and mumbled (complained) about responses that I would give almost anything to have back.

By contrast collectively this past quarter of the year has just flown by at the speed of light. As I struggle with the continued growth and treatment of my own cancer, these three months represents about one-third of the time my oncologist forecasts that I might expect to have left based upon my current trend. While I know that my life is in our Lord's hands, I can feel various parts of my body in outright mutiny, perhaps Gods way of continuing to prepare me for this next, perhaps final, season that lies in front of me.

We all experience life in seasons and rarely are any two seasons the same. Experience has taught me that if these periods in our life are similar, it is likely because our learning through the season has been slower than what was needed to properly manage the opportunities before us at that time. We all have good seasons and bad seasons, seasons that are hard and easy, fruitful, and stingy, prosperous and empty, full of love and heartache. The question that has been circulating in my head the past few weeks is related to the significance of these seasons. Are some seasons more important than others? Was having children more noteworthy than starting or selling a business? Were my seasons of recklessness in the eighties what prepared me for accepting the gifts and promises offered by my Creator and Savior? Wouldn't my life have been vastly different if I had not had a football-ending injury my senior year and accepted a job in Dallas?

When I look back for perspective, every one of these seasons had some defining impact that led to a new season with new dreams, hopes, and opportunities. And of course, all of this takes me into this final earthly season now well underway. What are the opportunities that lie ahead? Will this be the most important season or the least, or somewhere in the middle? What changes do I need to make to maximize the experiences that are coming at me rapid fire.

I am asking a lot of questions but don't have many answers especially answers that don't begin with "But God." I intend to do my best (better) to transparently share my heart and head as I walk this final narrow path. Most of you that read my Facebook posts have shared one or more of life's seasons with me, and my new friends are already partnering with me through your prayers and encouragement. Please pray that I would have wisdom and strength to finish well.

December 2, 2021

This past Tuesday night my beloved Duke Blue Devils played Ohio State in a late game. My son Ivan called early Tuesday saying that we had not yet watched a Duke game together and that he was going to come down (a thirty-minute drive) and watch the game. This is just one example of the way my children and friends have been intentional about making time to spend with me. He knew it would be a late night and that their two young children would be up early on Wednesday. The game was frustrating because after taking a comfortable lead, they began to slump and didn't score a basket for the last five minutes or so of the game.

As we walked to his car, I told him, "You know what this means don't you?" He said, "You want your keys back, don't you?" As he was closing his door to drive off, I said, "Keep the key. I'm going to change the locks." As he drove away, I said a little prayer, asking the Lord to guide him home safely. This thought flashed through my head, what if something happened to him or to me? My last words to him would be about locking him out of my home. I know, it was an empty threat, but the principle is something that I need to think about, perhaps even prepare for.

What would I want my last words to my children, spouse, and friends to be? Would they be words of love? Words of encouragement? Words of faith? Something about values or legacy? That's a lot of concepts to work into a "last words" conversation, especially because you likely have different conversations with each family member or friend. When you combine the fact that death is typically very untimely, trying to figure out when to share our last words along with the practical words we need to say seems like a fool's errand, though I plan to guard myself against ending conversations on a negative note.

I have decided that instead of focusing on last words it might be more productive to build on memorable experiences and so that is the path I intend to take as long as the Lord lets me.

I pray that this season of celebrating the birth of our Savior brings you many memorable experiences.

The only remaining question I have is, "Does anybody know a good locksmith?"

December 16, 2021

The Bomgardners have always been a family of huggers, greeting our family and friends with a warm embrace and sending them on their way with a positive clutch that reinforces the relationships we have built. Last October (2020) our youngest (Charlie) was bringing his new girl-friend to baby Spikes birthday party, but she came with a warning from Charlie, "She is not a hugger, so please honor her request not to be hugged." This was the first hugging confrontation I can remember and internally it set off a few warning signs. It is one thing to be uncomfortable hugging but to make a point of refusing them seems a little over the top. Additionally, for those of you who really know how my twisted mind works, I took this as a personal challenge to help her overcome her phobia and was able to hold my hug with her for an extra, uncomfortable moment at the end of the afternoon. The warning signs were real, and she was never going to fit in with our family anyway.

Hugs, I never really thought that much about them and had always kind of kept them in the benign category of accepted routine, kind of like handshakes, salutes, bows, and the like. I never really put much significance behind hugs with the glorious exception of watching my grandchildren run to me for an "arms fully extended, cheek to cheek" hug every time I see them. These serve as a constant reminder and reinforcement of our shared unconditional love for each other. Their enthusiasm for loving me and mine for them makes me long to live another day. Their hugs are inspirational.

With Barbara's departure to heaven, now right at four months ago, I have learned a lot more about the significance of our hugs together, something that I foolishly underestimated and certainly took for granted for more than four decades. As we negotiated the paths of our life together, like everyone, we experienced trials, setbacks, disappointment, loss, and all kinds of struggles. We also were blessed with victories and gifts from God: watching our children grow into adults and work together to overcome the challenges in their lives as they raise their children and build their careers. I don't know how I missed it, but somewhere in these life-altering events there were times when Barbara and I came together and just held each other, tearfully as we prayed for help, comfort, wisdom, healing, and peace in hard times and with joy as we praised and thanked God for his blessings during the good times. It is the real-life picture of two becoming one that the Bible describes for marriage, and we were one when we held each other and cried out to the Lord.

I have come to believe that these were holy hugs as we stood together leaning on and into the promises and hope of our Creator. We could feel His presence. We have experienced the blessings of overcoming struggles and celebrating the victories and blessings. He was always with us.

Over these past four months I am surprised by how much I miss; how important these holy hugs were to my everyday worship and managing the pathway for my life. I have also learned that I can expand the circle of my holy hugs to family and friends, a twist on my last words. I have started to say a brief prayer, sometimes aloud and sometimes not, for the person I am hugging goodbye. My potentially last words are a blessing for them. My goal is to leave my friends and family with a holy hug.

My prayer for all of you during this season of celebrating the birth of our Savior is that you come to know and experience the blessings of sharing holy hugs with the people you love.

December 23, 2021

In March of 2020 I posted a sarcastic story about my hospital experience with COVID, closing with the observation and commitment of my faith that regardless of what gets thrown at me, "They can't steal my Joy".

I want to clarify that my position was not a Job-like challenge to keep throwing hardships in my direction, but that is kind of what the past twenty-one months have felt like. In addition to this thrilling COVID roller coaster ride with hands held high, the love of my life was diagnosed with pancreatic cancer in September (2020). She experienced multiple hospital stays, extended chemo treatments, and blood transfusions as we watched her body deteriorate quickly until she passed away on August 17. At the same time, my body was worn down from almost three years of chemo, and my blood stopped producing the cells that it needs. I had three separate hospital stays in April, lost twenty more pounds on top of the forty-five I had already lost and have moved my medication strategy to managing pain versus fighting cancer.

What or who is trying to steal your joy this Christmas as we celebrate the birth of our Savior. It reminds me of that car commercial in which Mathew McConaughey asks, "where does it go?" Is there some giant storage center somewhere that houses all the joy that has been lost over time, or does it just disappear as though it never existed? Once joy is lost, can we ever get it back? And where does joy come from anyway, what is the source? History has demonstrated that you can't purchase joy. Wealth is not a barometer for happiness or contentment. Those that try to steal your joy don't get to keep it or use it. Your joy has no real value to anyone else. We all recognize people who are full of joy, and sadly we also know people who lack joy. The contrast can be stark. None of us would choose to have a joyless life, at least I would hope not. So where do we find joy?

Luke records the birth of Jesus. An angel goes to the shepherds and says to them, "Do not be afraid. I bring you good news that will cause *great joy* for all the people. Today in the city of David a Savior has been born to you. He is the Messiah, the Lord" (Luke 2:10-11). The angel points to joy is a major by-product of the birth of Jesus, and he identifies Jesus as the source.

This is the good news for all of us. Jesus, centuries before we were even born, came to earth to show us the way, to grant eternal life, forgiveness of sins, comfort, peace, and JOY.

Christmas, as opposed to New Year's, is the perfect time to stop and take a personal inventory of your life. Do you feel comforted even when you are going through trials and struggles? Do you feel like you have a companion as you battle through the challenges of life? Are you at peace with yourself, your family, friends, and coworkers? Do you carry around the weight of all the mistakes and poor choices you've made? Is your life full of joy?

If you are challenged by these questions, you don't need a New Year's resolution. You just need a simple prayer, a conversation with God. In your prayer, tell Him that you are missing His promises of peace, comfort, forgiveness, and joy. Ask Him for wisdom ("If any of you lacks wisdom, you should ask God ... and it will be given to you" (James 1:5) about what you should do next. "Seek and you will find" (Mathew 7:7).

For Christmas this year I pray that you are filled with joy and at peace with your family. For those that are not quite there yet, I pray that you will seek these promises from our Creator.

Merry Christmas!

December 31, 2021

As we turn the page on 2021, I am happy to report that I am still here to turn the page and head down the home stretch. This has been a week of decision-making, and, following discussions with my family, I have decided that it is time for me to move to hospice care. My body is not supporting my desire to continue to fight the cancer with the poison, and I have reached a point of diminishing returns in my quest to harvest quality time to spend with my family and loved ones. The focus of my medical support is now on fighting pain and seeking comfort.

I have prayed with my family and am praying with friends for the Lord to take me now (quickly), though I fear my body is still strong enough to keep my heart beating for months. I am inviting all of you to pray that the Lord will rescue me and take me home ASAP and would reduce, or eliminate, the pain and anxiety that is beating me down.

Just the time and effort to write this little update has worn me out, which means that future posts are likely to be shorter and to the point.

Thank you all for the way you have walked through this struggle with Barbara and me. You have been and continue to be a real blessing in our lives.

I will love you eternally for that!

February 12, 2022

It's been more than six months since Barbara passed, and I've only communicated with my Facebook friends one time. There's a lot of reasons/excuses for not reaching out, but the truth is, most of them are related to apathy and loneliness. It's hard to share when you're not certain what you're feeling as you're going through it. That said, the Lord keeps calling me back to share something, and so we're going to begin ADVENTURE 2.0

Barbara did a great job of fulfilling her role. She got out quickly before me, without lingering, and moved on to prepare the way for me. Apparently, I must be difficult (never heard that before) because she's still not ready for me. I would like to clean up any misconceptions about that because I am more than ready for her. I don't know if there's something or some term for being surrounded by friends and loved ones while you're lonely, but if they don't have a name for it, someone needs to find it.

The first of February we, as a family, all decided that it was time for me to go to hospice care, which means I have daily interaction with the hospice nurses on site and daily at-home service.

I have a series of Christian Nigerian nurses, and while there are at times subtle communications challenges, their prayer through song and praise is angelic. We have had some incredible spirit-filled times together.

We pray for healing, comfort, joy, and that the Lord would take me quickly. Most of those prayers are being answered daily.

Today, I continue to ask for the same prayers, especially the one about sending me home. Aside from asking for a friend or two to come play some cards or games periodically, I don't have much to share.

Thank you for your prayers.

March 19, 2022

With great sadness and great joy, our dad is now cancer-free and has won eternal victory! He is now celebrating with our mom in heaven. Our hearts are broken with the loss of such an inspirational and remarkable man. Thank you to everyone who supported, encouraged, and loved on our family throughout our parent's cancer journey.

March 23, 2022

Michael Ivan Bomgardner

September 3, 1953–March 18, 2022

 Michael Ivan Bomgardner was welcomed into heaven on March 18, 2022. Mike had a six-year battle with cancer and fought hard until the very end. He was surrounded by his children and their spouses when he passed away. Mike was a man of deep faith, which he shared regularly and easily with everyone he met. A believer in God's assurance of eternal life for those who trust Jesus Christ as their Lord and Savior, Mike has claimed the victory Jesus won over death and joins the heavenly ranks.

 He was a beloved son, brother, husband, father, grandfather, and friend. He was the oldest of four children between George Ivan and Betty Jo Work and took his role of big brother to Sherri, Debbie, and Mark very seriously.

 Growing up in a military family, Mike moved frequently as a child. Though he was born in Topeka, Kansas, the Bomgardner family settled in Haddon Heights, New Jersey, where Mike distinguished himself as a multi-sport athlete. Mike attended Duke University where he played football and was co-captain of the team in 1974-75. He was able to maintain many deep relationships with teammates and friends from both high school and college. A member of the Iron Dukes, some of Mike's best memories were of gatherings at NCAA Tournament venues to watch his beloved Blue Devils compete for national championships in basketball.

 After graduating from Duke, Mike began a career in retail merchandising, working as a buyer at a department store chain based in Texas. He transitioned to the supplier side of the retail business in the 1980s, selling for a manufacturer's rep company called Vanguard Sales that he would later own. Through multiple mergers with other rep organizations, Vanguard eventually became Innovative Sales Group. Mike retired from Innovative in 2018 after a long and successful career. In the comments he made upon retirement he shared that the most important thing to him about having led his company was not the wins and losses, the money earned, or the accolades received, but rather, the many deep personal relationships he enjoyed with partners, employees, suppliers, and customers. It was important to Mike to do his part to make where he lived a better place, so he served many years on the Farmers Branch City Council.

Most important, Mike married the love of his life, Barbara Lynn. The two were side by side for forty-four years. Their marriage was truly blessed; they had an unbreakable bond, devotion to one another, and a love that continued to grow throughout their life together. They had two beautiful children, Allison Holt and Michael Ivan Jr., and later adopted a third child, Charles Otto, in 2020. Mike was an incredible father, always ready to listen and give advice, give encouragement to build our confidence, and make us laugh with his quick wit and unique sense of humor. His grandchildren brought him pure joy. Mike frequently took each granddaughter on one-on-one dates, which included lunch followed by dress shopping. He took the time to invest in each of them and pour as much love into them as possible since he knew his time was limited due to his cancer.

Mike and Barbara were long-time members of Valley View Christian Church where they both served in numerous leadership positions. In God's currency, a person is measured by the investment he makes in others for God's kingdom. Mike was an exceedingly selfless person, always generous with his money, his time, and his wisdom. Love God and love others was the principle Mike lived by.

Mike is survived by his children and their spouses, Allison and Dustin VanZandt; Ivan and Leah Bomgardner; Charles Bomgardner; and his grandchildren, Emilia Jean Bomgardner, Sadie Rose VanZandt, Shiloh Faye VanZandt, Michael Ivan Bomgardner III; his siblings and their spouses, Debbie and Steven Ginsberg, Mark and Debbie Bomgardner, and Steven and Michelle Little; and numerous nieces and nephews.

CPSIA information can be obtained
at www.ICGtesting.com
Printed in the USA
BVHW041012090423
662009BV00004B/127